FACES OF PRAISE!

Also by Carol M. Mackey

Sistergirl Devotions:
Keeping Jesus in the Mix on the Job

FACES OF PRAISE!

PHOTOS & GOSPEL INSPIRATIONS TO ENCOURAGE & UPLIFT

CAROL M. MACKEY

PHOTOS BY

B. JEFFREY GRANT-CLARK

FOREWORD BY KIRK FRANKLIN

Faith
Words

NASHVILLE NEW YORK

FaithWords
Hachette Book Group
1290 Avenue of the Americas, New York, NY 10104
faithwords.com
twitter.com/faithwords

First Edition: October 2017

FaithWords is a division of Hachette Book Group, Inc. The FaithWords name and logo are trademarks of Hachette Book Group, Inc.

The publisher is not responsible for websites (or their content) that are not owned by the publisher.

LCCN: 2017948546

ISBNs: 978-1-4789-1752-6 (hardcover), 978-1-4789-1751-9 (ebook)

Printed in the United States of America

LSC-C

10 9 8 7 6 5 4 3 2 1

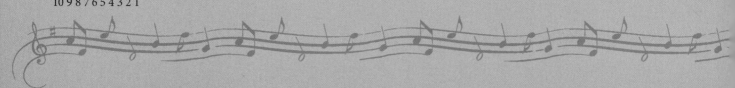

To my mom and dad—I miss you two every day.
Thank you for everything.
—Carol

To my amazing wife, Annette.
To all of the artists who allowed me to capture these images.
—B. Jeffrey

Contents

Contents

Contents

Contents

xv

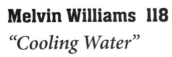

Contents

xvii

Foreword by KIRK FRANKLIN

When you dare to envision the imagery of the sacred, you must be willing to admit that passion and ambition are the lens you must choose to see that world through. Imagine the audacity one must have to attempt to photograph the spirit in midflight, a melody at its highest crescendo, or the reprise of a fatigued voice fighting to leave it all on the stage… What audacity.

There can be great pain in the middle of a song. A performance may reek of vulnerability. To let a camera invade that intimate moment of verse and chorus requires honesty, skill, professionalism, and trust. Benjamin's lens brings exactly that.

The images you see are of epic moments that might have been forgotten until seen again in this collection. This book is movement, artistry, ministry, and storytelling at its highest level.

All the artists know Benjamin. They've traveled with him, sought his counsel on their careers and tough family decisions. So when he attempts to capture their paintings of sound and emotion, they know they are in the hands of a friend, a brother, and a fellow artist.

The faces in this collection are of God's children. Their praise is to the Invisible Creator, whom the camera can't see. Yet somehow, Benjamin makes the invisible revealed. Look into their eyes in each picture. There God is…in every tear, every smile, every strain of the skin. When you open your eyes to these photos, feel God leaping off of the paper into your heart.

This collection succeeds on every level. Carol Mackey's devotional text perfectly complements the photos. How proud we are of this piece of history—our history, the gospel of color, courage, and community…the gospel of US.

Foreword by Kirk Franklin

FACES OF PRAISE!

Yolanda ADAMS

"The Battle Is the Lord's"

" 'You will not need to fight in this battle. Position yourselves, stand still and see the salvation of the LORD, who is with you, O Judah and Jerusalem!' Do not fear or be dismayed; tomorrow go out against them, for the LORD is with you."

2 CHRONICLES
20:17

Tests and trials will come in the life of every Christian. In John 16:33, Jesus warns, "In this world you will have tribulation. But be of good cheer, for I have overcome the world." Note that He didn't say "well, maybe" or "there's a good chance." He said you will have tribulation.

Now, that would scare just about all of us, because no one wants trouble. We want to avoid it at all costs. But He tells us to not worry about it because He's fighting our battle (2 Chronicles 20:15). Think of God as a big brother who comes to the school yard and confronts the bully who's been picking on you for months. More than likely, you won't have any more problems with your tormentor. One bigger, stronger, and more powerful has gotten in their face. So they retreat.

So it is with Jesus. He's at the right hand of the Father fighting our battles for us (Hebrews 12:2). He is our Big Brother, and Satan is the school-yard bully that He always keeps on a very short leash. Listen to Yolanda Adams' reassuring song and meditate on this verse. The Lord will fight your battle—you have nothing to fear.

HIGH NOTE:
The Lord is ready to war on your behalf. Turn your battles over to Him.

Yolanda Adams 𝄞 *"The Battle Is the Lord's"*

Shari ADDISON

"Please Make Me Better"

> "O house of Israel,
> can I not do with you as this potter?" says the LORD.
> "Look, as the clay is in the potter's hand,
> so are you in My hand, O house of Israel!"

JEREMIAH 18:6

Every Christian is a "work in progress." Although I've been a believer for over thirty years, there are some things I still struggle with. I've read the Bible, I believe the Bible, I try my very best to live the Bible (James 1:22). But with all of that, I know I have areas of my life that the Lord needs to work on.

No one has reached godly perfection except Jesus—and He was born that way! Unfortunately our sin "gene" prevents earthly perfection. Even Paul, the "super apostle," admitted that he had a problem with bragging (2 Corinthians 12:6). And the Lord gave him a "thorn in the flesh"—a gentle reminder to keep him humble (v. 7). Scripture doesn't reveal what that "thorn" was, but my guess is it wasn't good since he asked the Lord to remove it (v. 8). Paul got the same answer all three times he asked: no.

At the time, Paul didn't know that his thorn was making him better. Like most of us, he just wanted the problem to go away. As he endured pain and hardship, he turned from the tendency to brag about his achievements in the ministry to bragging about Jesus' accomplishments in him. Quite a turnaround. God loves us so much that He uses our trials to get us to where we need to be. The ultimate goal is to become more and more like Jesus.

HIGH NOTE:
The Lord is making me better day by day.

Shari Addison ♪ "Please Make Me Better"

Crystal AIKIN

"I Desire More"

> Delight yourself also in the Lord,
> and He shall give you the desires of your heart.
>
>
>
> PSALM 37:4

*I*s your desire more of God? That means study His Word to learn His ways, who He is, and His promises to us. A wonderful thing about God is that if you ask for more of Him, He delivers right away.

You may need Him to help you with a tough decision. He will give you the wisdom to make the right choice. It may be a Scripture, a line in a book you're reading, or wise words your grandchild utters. God has no set way of pouring into us; that's why we can't put Him in a box.

We can be laser focused on everything other than God and forget that the Problem Solver can provide us with all we need, if we just slow down and ask. There have been times when I've spun my wheels and worked myself into a tizzy trying to figure things out without ever thinking to consult God. Finally, after running into wall after wall, I'd have an "aha!" moment from God. He was always there, waiting to help me, but I brushed right past Him. I do that less and less these days, as I learn to desire God more.

God wants you to want Him. As Crystal Aikin sings, *Not my will but your will. Less of me and more of you*. When we decrease (put less focus on ourselves), He will increase in our lives. And the blessings will multiply. I don't know about you, but I like that math!

HIGH NOTE:
God always gives you more than you expect when you seek Him first.

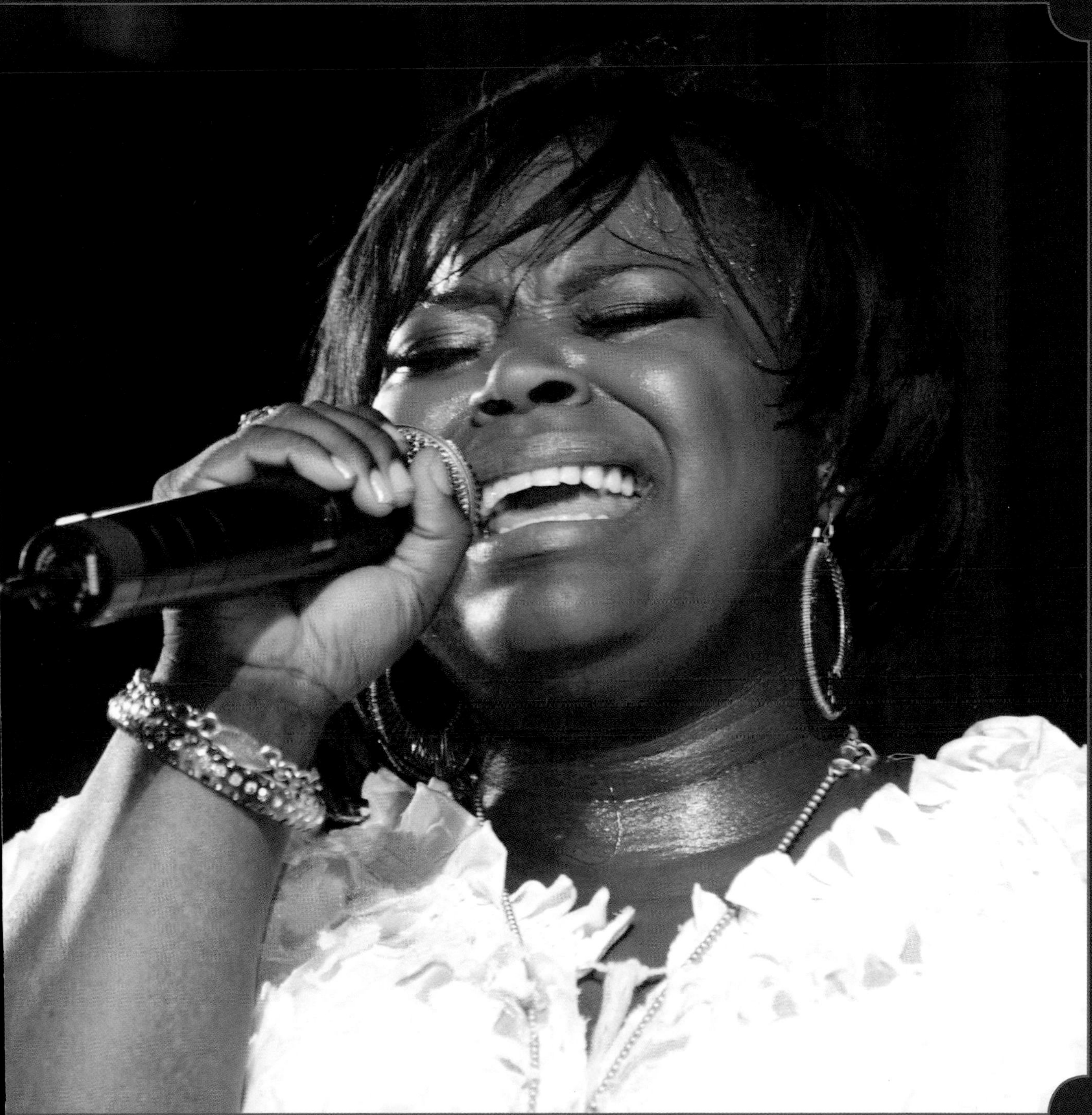

Rance ALLEN

"You That I Trust"

The Lord is my rock and my fortress and my deliverer;
my God, my strength, in whom I will trust;
my shield and the horn of my salvation, my stronghold.

PSALM 18:2

The Bible says that God has given everyone a measure of faith (Romans 12:3), even if that faith is as small as a mustard seed (Matthew 17:20). With that faith comes trust, the identical twin of faith.

We trust that God is who He says He is. We trust that the Bible is true. We trust that God sent His only begotten Son to save us from our sins. We trust that Jesus is sitting at the right hand of the Father. We trust that God cannot lie (Numbers 23:19), that He will keep His word.

It's important to God that we trust Him. Sometimes He will give us small things to trust Him with so that we will learn to trust Him with big things. As our faith develops, our trust will grow.

It hurts God when we don't trust Him. When someone betrays our trust, we are heartbroken and feel violated. Think about how you'd feel if friends hid their valuables when you visited them. Or your coworker "double-checked" every project you worked on together. Or your spouse checked your text and phone log or put a tracking device on your car. It would take a long time to trust them again, if ever. Trust is key in our relationships with people—and most importantly with God. We must trust God with everything that concerns us. He will deliver us, provide for us, comfort us, and carry us through any challenge that comes our way. Trust is the key!

HIGH NOTE:
You can trust God. He'll do what He says He will do!

Vanessa Bell ARMSTRONG

"Peace Be Still"

> Then He arose and rebuked the wind,
> and said to the sea, "Peace, be still!"
> And the wind ceased, and there was a great calm.
>
> MARK 4:39

During storms, lightning flashes in the sky, thunder roars, umbrellas turn inside out from strong winds, streets flood, and trees can snap in two. The stormy periods in our lives are just like that—messy and inconvenient. Dark clouds hover over us for what seems like an eternity. We pray, we fast, and we wonder if the sun will ever shine again.

The Lord's disciples thought for sure they were going to die in a little windswept boat one rainy night. Terrified, they woke Jesus from his nap (Mark 4:37–38). I imagine he yawned, stretched, and surveyed his wet and shaken compadres. He probably shook his head. Poor things. Their faith wasn't there yet. They didn't yet know that when HE was on the scene, everything would be all right. There would be no drowning. Not that day. Not on his watch. So He probably looked at the turbulence, held up His hand, and ordered the waves to knock it off—now. Scripture says that immediately "there was a great calm" (v. 39).

No matter what kind of rainy season you're experiencing—a long, torrential downpour or a sun shower—it matters to Jesus. His protective arm is wrapped around your shoulder, holding you close until the storm passes and it's bright and sunny in your life again.

HIGH NOTE:
Jesus is your peace. You can trust Him with your storm.

Vanessa Bell Armstrong 𝄞 *"Peace Be Still"*

Amber BULLOCK
"Lord You've Been So Good"

> Oh, taste and see that the LORD is good;
> blessed is the man who trusts in Him!
>
>
>
> PSALM 34:8

I love to hear the older Christians testify in church. These seasoned saints may close their eyes, raise their hand, or "do a lil' step" to pay homage to their King, uttering, "When I think about the goodness of Jesus and all He's brought me through…" It's been said, "There's no testimony without a test." It's evident that they have been tried in the fire.

Quite often, I get quiet and just think about how the Lord has blessed me. I take for granted (and shouldn't) being able to walk, talk, work, etcetera, and in those quiet times I realize, as the old folks say, "I coulda been dead and sleeping in my grave." But Jesus came to the rescue, saving, delivering, protecting, providing. He's truly good—in all these ways!

He **protects** you: "I am the good shepherd. The good shepherd gives His life for the sheep" (John 10:11).

He **cares** for you: "But when He saw the multitudes, He was moved with compassion for them, because they were weary and scattered, like sheep having no shepherd" (Matthew 9:36).

He **comforts** you: "When the Lord saw her, He had compassion on her and said to her, 'Do not weep'" (Luke 7:13).

He **heals** you: "And by His stripes we are healed" (Isaiah 53:5).

He **provides** for you: "Look at the birds of the air, for they neither sow nor reap nor gather into barns; yet your heavenly Father feeds them. Are you not of more value than they?" (Matthew 6:26).

HIGH NOTE:
Be thankful for the Lord's tender mercies. They are new every day.

Amber Bullock   *"Lord You've Been So Good"*

Kim BURRELL

"I Come to You More than I Give"

Bless the LORD, O my soul,
and forget not all His benefits.

PSALM 103:2

When it comes time for us to pray, we find other things to ask for, instead of giving thanks for what God has already done. Although Kim Burrell's velvety voice is soothing, her lyrics are convicting. Why? Because they are true.

As much as I love uplifting, spirit-boosting gospel songs, sometimes we need a not-so-gentle reminder of where we may be "missing it" with God.

We give God our laundry list of requests: "Lord, please fix this, please heal that, and gimme..." We babble on and throw in a "thank you, Jesus" at the end, for good measure. I'm guilty of this, at times, especially when needs are critical. But that's no excuse. No wonder Jesus referred to us as "children," and in some instances "little children." Even mature believers can act like spiritual toddlers. Rarely will kids say, "Mom/Dad, thank you for the roof over our heads, food on our table, and clothes on our backs." No, they dive right in and ask, "Can I have money to go shopping?" We do the same thing with God.

When we offer the God of all creation no praise or gratitude for our blessings, we short-change Him. Prayer is an act of worship. Imagine how God feels when we start with requests rather than thanks. He doesn't need our praise—the rocks will cry out if we don't praise Him (Luke 19:40). He wants and enjoys our praise! Neither does the God of the universe need our "honey do" lists. He knows what we need before we open our mouths (Matthew 6:8).

HIGH NOTE:

God wants us to praise Him in good and bad times.

Kim Burrell ♪ *"I Come to You More than I Give"*

15

Jonathan BUTLER

"I Stand on Your Word"

> As for God, His way is perfect;
> the word of the LORD is proven;
> He is a shield to all who trust in Him.

2 SAMUEL 22:31

Even the most trustworthy and well-meaning person may let you down. We've all been guilty of breaking our words. But the good news is, whether you're a promise keeper or struggle with your commitments, God's Word is infallible. His Word is above all. Jesus says in Mark 13:31 that "Heaven and earth will pass away, but My words will by no means pass away." That's a pretty big statement. His Word takes precedence over what He created!

God cannot lie (Titus 1:2), so when He makes a promise, it holds weight. When you read the Bible, from the creation story in Genesis to the end-time prophecy in Revelation, you see God's faithfulness. He wants you to rely on His promises—not your feelings. When you "feel" like a failure, God says you are more than a conqueror (Romans 8:37). When you "feel" God has abandoned you, God says He'll never leave you (Hebrews 13:5).

As Jonathan Butler sings, *Even when my faith is weary, I believe.* There may be times when you read your Bible till you're cross-eyed, pray until you're hoarse, fast until you're weak, and you still may not see a change in your situation. You're ready to throw in the towel and give up on God. But remember, He's the same God who raised Jesus from the dead on the third day. I'm sure it looked hopeless those first two days. But what God said came to pass. If He said it, He will do it!

HIGH NOTE:
You can take God at His Word.

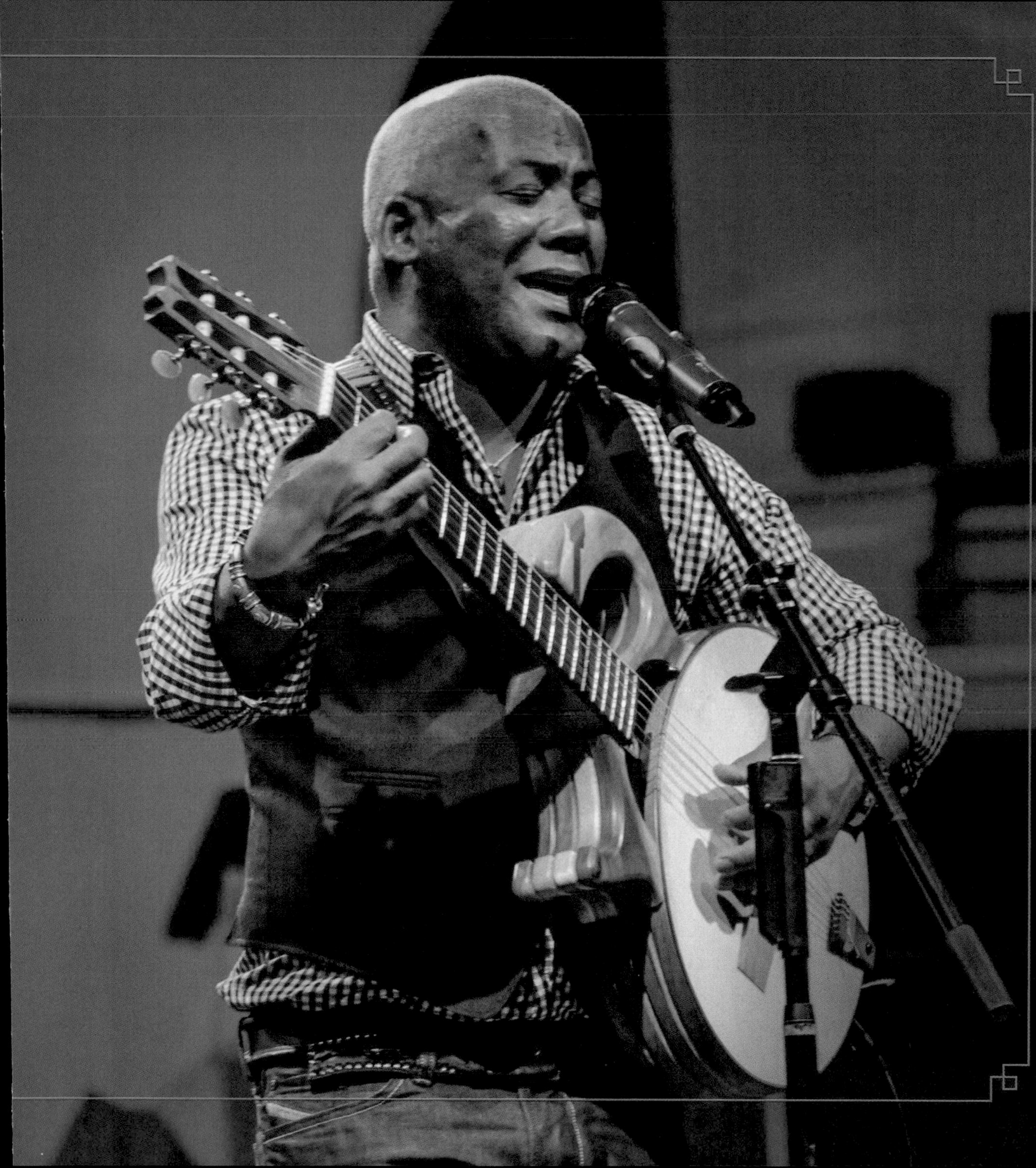

Myron BUTLER

"Bless the Lord"

> Bless the LORD, O my soul;
> and all that is within me, bless His holy name!
> Bless the LORD, O my soul,
> and forget not all His benefits.

PSALM 103:1–2

My mom eased into eternity in 2014. I signed her into hospice just days after I was laid off from my job of sixteen years. Litigation was pending for a nasty divorce. After those zingers, my mother's death made me numb. As I was getting dressed for her wake, "Bless the Lord" was playing in the background. I turned it up.

The funeral director wanted the kids to view the body before visitors arrived, and I was already late. My siblings were waiting. I was in no rush to face the reality of my mother's death. I took my sweet time. *Bless the Lord, oh my soul and all that is within me…* I sang loudly, as tears streamed down my face. It had finally hit me. My mom was gone.

I put on my black dress and heels, all the while thinking about how God had kept me during the months when my life had began to unravel. Fresh tears flowed as I reflected on His goodness. I was late to that wake for a reason. I needed that time to be alone with God to thank Him—to bless Him with my mouth, my heart, and my spirit. In that blessing was incredible healing and strength I knew came only from Him.

HIGH NOTE:
God is our strength when we are at our weakest point.

Myron Butler ♪ *"Bless the Lord"*

Shirley CAESAR

"Good God"

Oh, give thanks to the LORD, for He is good!
For His mercy endures forever.

PSALM 118:1

A frantic phone call woke us up in 2001 on the morning of September 11th. We were in Atlantic City celebrating my fortieth birthday that weekend. "A plane just crashed into the Twin Towers—turn on the TV!" my husband's friend screeched through the phone. Seconds after we turned it on, the second plane crashed through the other tower.

The hotel was being evacuated, so we were quickly getting ready to go back to New York, when I remembered: my brother John had been on a temp assignment for the past six months in the World Trade Center. I slid down the granite shower stall, weeping. I was sure he was dead. As I was getting dressed, I tried every few minutes to call him. Like so many others that morning, I only received an erratic busy signal. Then finally, I heard a disconnect message. I was in shock.

We were unable to return to the city because all bridges and tunnels were shut down, so we stopped at a diner. I couldn't eat. A lump was in my throat. I tried, but my eggs wouldn't go down. This is what it feels like when someone you love dies, I thought.

My phone rang. It was my sister Joan. I picked it up right away and before I could utter "hello" she said, "John's ok!" He had escaped before the tower he worked in collapsed.

"Thank you, Jesus!" I never felt such relief in all my life. I closed my eyes and prayed. God had spared my family enormous grief. I will certainly "never forget" His goodness.

HIGH NOTE:
God is more than good. God is *great*.

Shirley Caesar ♪ *"Good God"*

Byron CAGE

"The Presence of the Lord Is Here"

> Lo, I am with you always,
> even to the end of the age.
>
>
>
> MATTHEW
> 28:20

*T*he Spirit of the Lord is here, the Spirit of the Lord is here, I feel it in the atmosphere, the Spirit of the Lord is here…So goes Byron Cage's exuberant praise song. There's nothing like corporate praise and worship. Whether it's in a megachurch or a storefront, a Christian conference or a small prayer circle, God says where two or more are gathered in His name, there He is in the midst of them (Matthew 18:20).

And when God shows up, He shows out!

Even when it doesn't feel like it, God's presence is always with us—He is always with us. It doesn't matter how we feel. We can be ecstatically happy or feeling low. His presence is still with us.

That's why it's important to not depend solely on whether or not you feel God's presence. He doesn't always operate in the spectacular. Sometimes He speaks to us in whispers, as we are washing the dishes, or He may surprise us with a special notecard from an old friend. We'd all like to experience the physical presence of God (whom we can't see), but you may totally miss God—and your blessing—if you're seeking a "feeling."

HIGH NOTE:

God's presence is always with you because He is always with you.

Byron Cage ♭ *"The Presence of the Lord Is Here"*

Erica CAMPBELL

"A Little More Jesus"

> My brethren, count it all joy
> when you fall into various trials,
> knowing that the testing of your faith
> produces patience.

JAMES 1:2–3

*W*here are your nerves worked the most? Probably on the job. The workplace is almost always where you need a little more Jesus, sometimes a lot more of Him!

In my first book, *Sistergirl Devotions: Keeping Jesus in the Mix on the Job*, I recount some of my own unpleasant situations at work and how had it not been for the Holy Spirit keeping me in check, I could have destroyed my witness—and gotten fired. One such instance happened during a salary review for my staff. My boss handed me the reviews and annual increases of the senior staff members I'd recently been asked to supervise. Both of my direct reports were making more money than me! It was one of my angriest moments at work, but I thank God for His wisdom. Things could have gotten ugly.

The Holy Spirit led me to research comparable salaries for my title and experience. One of my mentors, a top executive at a major entertainment company, coached me on how to present my case. I did and got my salary adjustment. I thank God for His guidance—it led to a blessing.

When I first heard Erica Campbell's hit "A Little More Jesus," I was reminded that I sure do need more Jesus in every workplace situation.

HIGH NOTE:
Whether you need a little more Jesus, or a lot more, He's always there.

Kurt CARR

"I've Seen Him Do It"

If two of you agree on earth concerning anything that they ask, it will be done for them by My Father in heaven.

MATTHEW
18:19

*W*hen you're in a crisis, hurt, confused, don't understand what you're going through (or why), and can't see clearly to the other side—even after you've prayed for deliverance— you begin to lose hope when God remains silent. Then you meet someone who's overcome the same obstacle you're struggling with. It gives you comfort. You never suffer alone. The Lord won't let that happen. He loves you too much. *He can turn the mess you're in into an awesome miracle. I know He can. I've seen Him do it.*

During my divorce, many women (and men) told me how God brought them out onto the other side. "You will get through this," they assured me, sometimes through tears. Their words soothed my tired soul. The lyrics to Kurt Carr's song relate God's modern-day miracles. Kurt gives a powerful testimony about his mother's miraculous healing from lung cancer. What enormous hope for any cancer patient!

Did God show up for you when you needed Him most? Tell others. Share how you got through it and assure them that they will, too. I love *The Message* version of 2 Corinthians 1:4: "He comes alongside us when we go through hard times, and before you know it, he brings us alongside someone else who is going through hard times so that we can be there for that person just as God was there for us."

HIGH NOTE:

God will use your pain to help others who are hurting.

Kurt Carr & *"I've Seen Him Do It"*

Jacky CLARK-CHISHOLM

"My Season"

> There is a season (a time appointed) for everything and a time for every delight and event or purpose under heaven.
>
>
>
> ECCLESIASTES
> 3:1 (AMP)

My brother John is not only a strong Christian, he's a wise man. During two of my toughest years, I'd often call John for a pick-me-up. "Carol, everybody gets a turn," he'd say.

Why was my "turn" happening now, at seemingly the worst time in my life? I didn't understand it. I felt like a failure. But something great came out of that difficult period: an abundance of God's grace and mercy. I was still pummeled by my storm, but little, unexpected blessings gave me new hope that better days were coming. One thing that challenging period taught me was that everything is cyclical. Seasons change and so do circumstances. The Holy Spirit, in His goodness, brought back to my attention the seasons in my life that yielded a bumper crop of blessings: publication of my first book, a stellar career, numerous awards for my work in African American publishing, ritzy vacations to South Beach and Martha's Vineyard, my first business trip abroad—and too many more to list. In that lush, green season of my life, as my dad would say, I "wasn't feeling no pain!" I smiled at the memory, and God promised there would be more. Bad times taught me to always remember the great seasons.

God gave me this takeaway: Stormy seasons have an expiration date. Ride it out. It will pass. Your lush, green season is coming. Jacky Clark-Chisholm's song affirms it: *Happy days are here again, the crying's done, the verdict's in.* Best of all, God promises it (Psalm 1:3)!

HIGH NOTE:
The Lord helps you weather the seasons in life.

Jacky Clark-Chisholm ♪ *"My Season"*

Dorinda CLARK-COLE

"I'm Still Here"

> The LORD will preserve him and keep him alive,
> and he will be blessed on the earth;
> You will not deliver him to the will of his enemies.

PSALM 41:2

The chorus to this song is a constant reminder of God's goodness. Can you remember instances of the Lord's saving grace? I certainly do. When my ex-husband and I were a young couple with two preschool sons, we were financially in over our heads. We got behind on the mortgage and finally our house went into foreclosure. I dabbed tears as the movers carried our furniture to the street. (My in-laws had already taken the boys to their house in the next town. We didn't want them to see this.) As the sheriff was sealing the house, my ex sat at the curb in his easy chair to make sure no one stole our belongings. As the moving van pulled off with our furniture, we walked the mile to his parents' house. (The car had already been repossessed.) We had hit rock bottom. I was too hurt to be embarrassed.

When one of my friends said, "People lose their mind over stuff like that. Some even commit suicide," I was too numb to say anything. But in my heart, I knew God was keeping me from losing my mind, or worse yet, my faith. Had it not been for His mercy and grace, I may have been one of those desperate souls. Now I can shout my testimony from the rooftop and say that I'm still here and it's by the grace of God! As tough as it seemed at the time, I experienced a "spiritual growth spurt" and total restoration. Great faith came out of a bad situation.

HIGH NOTE:
You may have had it rough—but you're still here!

Dorinda Clark-Cole 𝄞 *"I'm Still Here"*

Tasha COBBS

"Break Every Chain"

> Then they cried out to the LORD in their trouble,
> and He saved them out of their distresses.
> He brought them out of darkness and the shadow of death,
> and broke their chains in pieces.
>
>
>
> PSALM 107:13–14

"Break Every Chain" is not only a powerful praise song but an anthem of victory! Jesus has come to set us free from all that is intended to bind us and hold us hostage—emotional scars, financial lack, bad relationships, and poor health, to name a few. In 2 Corinthians 4:13, we are reminded that if we believe, we must also speak. Memorize the verses from the Chain-Breaking Affirmations on the next pages that pertain to your situation so you are always ready to speak that Scripture.

Isaiah 42:3 says, "A bruised reed He will not break." In 2 Timothy 2:3 we read, "You therefore must endure hardship as a good soldier of Jesus Christ." God will preserve you for His divine purpose. You will make it through!

HIGH NOTE:
No chains can hold you! Jesus can break every chain in your life.

Tasha Cobbs & "Break Every Chain"

Chain-Breaking Affirmations

God loves me unconditionally.

    John 3:16

    Deuteronomy 23:5

    John 16:27

I walk by faith, not by sight.

    2 Corinthians 5:7

    2 Corinthians 4:18

    Hebrews 11:1

I rise above my circumstances. God is arranging things in my favor.

    Ephesians 1:11

    Romans 8:28

    Psalm 27:14

God is my total Source. I lack nothing.

    Psalm 122:7

    Psalm 1:3

    Matthew 6:30

My enemies have no power over me.

    Psalm 37:7

    Romans 8:31

    Psalm 18:37–38

I am an overcomer through Christ Jesus.

    Matthew 12:20

    1 John 5:4–5

    1 Corinthians 15:57

My joy comes from the Lord.

    Psalm 16:11

    Nehemiah 8:10

    John 15:11

I am healed.

    Jeremiah 17:14

    Psalm 30:2

    Psalm 103:2–3

    Isaiah 53:5

    Psalm 118:17

I break the chains of depression.

    Psalm 147:3

    2 Corinthians 10:4

    Matthew 12:20

    Psalm 30:5

    Isaiah 61:3

My prayers are powerful and effective.

    Proverbs 15:29

    Psalm 6:9

    Matthew 21:22

    James 5:16

Joann ROSARIO CONDREY

"I Hear You Say"

My son, give attention to my words;
incline your ear to my sayings.

PROVERBS 4:20

When God speaks, I listen. Whichever way He chooses to communicate with my spirit, whether it's the "still, small voice," His Word, or through a gifted believer, I take heed. If the Most High God loves me enough to reach down from heaven to give me a special word, it must be important. I want my spiritual ears to be as clean as my natural ones—with no wax buildup!

Moses listened to God when He gave him the Ten Commandments. Mary listened to the angel who told her she would give birth to the Savior of the world. Paul listened to Jesus on the road to Damascus.

So many voices seek to mimic God's; it's easy to get fooled. So pray for discernment. One sure-fire way to know if a message is from God is that He will never contradict His Word (Isaiah 55:11). Believers who manifest spiritual gifts to "give us a word" are vessels of God, using their gift to His glory. "The voice of the LORD is powerful; the voice of the LORD is full of majesty" (Psalm 29:4).

Psychics work through "familiar spirits" (Leviticus 19:31). Satan is the chief counterfeiter of everything pure and godly. The devil is full of contradictions. He's the original Liar and the truth is not in him (John 8:44). So we must be careful about chasing down someone to "give us a word."

The Lord has more than one way to speak to you. Keep your ears and heart open. Don't box God in. And of course, Jesus is always of one accord with the Father, and He wants us to be too.

HIGH NOTE:
God is always listening and He hopes you are, too.

Joann Rosario Condrey ♪ *"I Hear You Say"*

Let's Pray

Father God, I come to You humbly, asking You, Lord, to give me ears to hear. Your Word says that Your sheep hear Your voice and the voice of another they will not follow. I want Your voice to be the only one I hear when I have issues that trouble me. In Jesus' name I pray. Amen.

Joann Rosario Condrey 𝄞 *"I Hear You Say"*

Y'Anna CRAWLEY

"Grandma's Hands"

> I call to remembrance the genuine faith that is in you,
> which dwelt first in your grandmother Lois and your mother Eunice,
> and I am persuaded is in you also.
>
> 2 TIMOTHY 1:5

*I*first heard "Grandma's Hands" when Bill Withers recorded it in 1971, long before this upbeat gospel rendition. The song came to mind just days after my own grandmother's death. I burst into tears as I recalled her twisted, arthritic hands. Grandma lived in a small town outside of Columbia, South Carolina. Our family made it down there from New York every few years. Although I didn't see much of her, I loved hearing her stories, brushing her black hair, so long that she could sit on it, and laughing at all the good-natured jabs she'd take at my mother. We had great times on her front porch those hot summer days.

Many grandmothers I talk to love their role because they can spoil the grands rotten and, as one woman chuckled, "then send them home to their parents." However, not every family dynamic is the same. Some grandmothers have to step into the role of mother and raise their grandchildren. "Grandma" becomes "Momma." If you were raised by a God-fearing grandmother who took you to church, taught you how to pray, and instilled in you Christian principles and godly values, you are blessed.

One of my pastors admonished the young mothers in our church, "You are not only raising your children, you're raising your grandchildren." He meant that what we teach our children, they will teach their children. So if you're a grandmother, your godly example will have an impact on the children in your family.

HIGH NOTE:
Grandmothers have a special place in our hearts—and God's.

Y'Anna Crawley & *"Grandma's Hands"*

Andraé CROUCH

"Through It All"

> You therefore must endure hardship as a good soldier of Jesus Christ.
>
> 2 TIMOTHY 2:3

*P*astor Andraé Crouch was one of the greatest gospel artists of all time. When he passed in early 2015, the whole world mourned. Like so many of us, Andraé Crouch experienced his share of trials. In "Through It All" he thanks God for seeing him through his most difficult days: *God gave me blessed consolation that my trials come to only make me strong.*

I once heard a pastor say, "You're either in something, coming out of something, or getting ready to go back into something." Our lives won't stay in "neutral" for long. Hardship and tough times will come.

The Bible character Job lost his health, children, and livelihood. When he didn't curse God for what he was going through, his wife turned her back on him. But at the end of his testing period, his blessings were also extreme. The Lord blessed him with twice as much as he had before his trial (Job 42:10).

As we look back on our lives, we will see that even in the shakiest circumstances, we had something to be thankful for. You may have lost your job but the rent got paid every month. Despite your depleted savings, your child's college tuition got paid every semester. God came through while you were going through!

HIGH NOTE:

We can depend on Jesus through it all.

Kirk FRANKLIN

"I Smile"

A merry heart makes a cheerful countenance.

**PROVERBS
15:13**

People have always told me, "Carol. You have the prettiest smile," and "Your smile lights up a room." I graciously thank them, and while I'm flattered, the truth of the matter is sometimes it's hard to smile. Some church folk seem to think you should go around grinning like a Cheshire cat even when you're going through the hardest times of your life, but that reads as fake and people will think you've escaped from a psych ward. There are times when the last thing we want to do is smile.

The year I divorced, I lost my job and my mother was dying—the weight of those events all happening at once sought to grind me to powder. There were times I thought I'd collapse under the stress, but God wrapped me in His loving arms. As Kirk Franklin's chorus sings, *I almost gave up, but a power that I can't explain fell from heaven like a shower now.* Though the pain was etched on my face, I could still muster a smile. I wasn't my usual cheery self, but my smile reflected my heart.

My smile during that rough season of my life was certainly not of my making. It was God's. The love of Christ gave me joy and compelled me to smile even when my world was falling apart.

HIGH NOTE:
You can smile in the midst of adversity because your joy comes from the Lord.

Kirk Franklin ♪ "I Smile"

Travis GREENE

"Intentional"

And we know that all things work together for good
to those who love God,
to those who are the called according to His purpose.

ROMANS 8:28

All things are working for my good because He's intentional, never failing…I don't have to worry 'cause it's working for me. Travis Greene is absolutely right: God is intentional in everything. God has a purpose behind all He says and does. He laid the foundation for humanity, for "the world and those who dwell therein" (Psalm 24:1). God is not wishy-washy, scratching His head, trying to figure out His next move. He knows exactly what His next move is.

When it comes to our lives, the same is true. He doesn't toss dice. He has plans for us. Just as no two people on earth have the same fingerprints, no two people have the exact same plan for their lives.

God's plan is perfect for you (Jeremiah 29:11). Don't get discouraged when your life doesn't go according to how you think it should. Sometimes the Lord allows detours, delays, and setbacks as opportunities for you to learn and grow. But nothing can stop His plan for your life. Time can't, people can't. And circumstances won't. Your blessings, your purpose, your anointing, your calling—all of it is handcrafted specifically for you by your Creator, and no one else.

He's intentional and you should be too:

- Be intentional in your worship. • Be intentional in your giving. • Be intentional in your marriage.
- Be intentional in your commitments. • Be intentional in your relationship with God.

HIGH NOTE:
God's plan for your life is perfect. All things are working for your good!

Travis Greene ♪ "Intentional"

Deitrick HADDON

"Well Done"

> His lord said to him,
> "Well done, good and faithful servant;
> you were faithful over a few things,
> I will make you ruler over many things.
> Enter into the joy of your lord."

MATTHEW
25:21

*W*ell done, good and faithful servant." Those are the sweetest words we can hear when we stand face-to-face with the Master. Like an excellent student, we want an A+. Like an exemplary employee, we want that promotion. As a servant of the Most High God, we want the reward of entry into God's Kingdom. It is the ultimate pat on the back. It's everything. Our relationship with God through Jesus Christ will determine if we get that final welcome or miss heaven altogether—and none of us want that!

So many get confused, thinking service to God is limited to inside church walls. Truth is, your ministry expands outside of the church. It's in your home, on your job, in your community, and in your relationships. Every role is important and necessary for a church to operate successfully, but in-house ministry is only part of our service to God. In "Well Done" Deitrick Haddon sings, *I don't want my singing Lord, I don't want it to be in vain*. None of us want our service to God to be ineffective or a waste of time. Our witness should touch lives and bring people into relationship with Jesus Christ.

Serve people. Be committed and faithful to whatever purpose God has for your life (1 Corinthians 4:2) so you can get the ultimate "thumbs-up" from the Lord: "Well done!"

HIGH NOTE:
There is a prize waiting for us in heaven—His name is Jesus!

Deitrick Haddon ♭ *"Well Done"*

Deitrick Haddon 𝄞 *"Well Done"*

J. J. HAIRSTON

"After This"

For our light affliction,
which is but for a moment,
is working for us
a far more exceeding
and eternal weight of glory.

2 CORINTHIANS
4:17

I love this song because it's about hanging on to hope—even if by a thread—and looking *past* your current situation, not looking *at* it. Your circumstance may be dire. Things don't look good.

Maybe it's a biased judge in your child custody case. You've been scheduled to undergo yet another round of chemotherapy. A long bout of unemployment has depleted the last of your savings. Setback after setback, trial after trial, you wonder if this nightmare is your "new normal" and if it will ever end. You may feel confused and feel like God has abandoned you.

The lyrics in this empowering song provide hope: *God specializes in things impossible, He loves to move when all hope is lost, just so He can show Himself strong on your behalf. Don't give up, He'll come through for you!* It may not look or feel like it now, but there will be an "after this" to your ordeal. And then you will shout praise from the rooftops! God gets glory when He brings us out of a tough battle. When we can stand up in church and "testify" to His goodness, we encourage other Christians who may be going through tough times.

As the words to the song affirm: Your trial is temporary. It will end.

HIGH NOTE:

Don't you dare give up!

J. J. Hairston & *"After This"*

Fred HAMMOND
"No Weapon"

> "But in that coming day no weapon turned against you will succeed.
> You will silence every voice raised up to accuse you.
> These benefits are enjoyed by the servants of the LORD;
> their vindication will come from me.
> I, the LORD, have spoken!"

ISAIAH 54:17
(NLT)

*W*ords can lift you up, encourage you, inspire you, and motivate you. We all love to be around positive people who speak life into us and over us. But some folks use words as weapons—and they hurt worse than if we'd been sucker punched.

If you've ever gotten a promotion on the job, in ministry, or in an organization, you know that not everyone was happy for you. You might see it in their body language, but you certainly heard them speak their true feelings in backhanded compliments or thinly veiled insults followed by "You know I'm just kidding!" They murder you with their mouth. Jealousy is a green-eyed monster, and you'll get your share of it if you have a spirit of excellence (Daniel 6:3). People may tell lies and gossip about you and try to sully your name.

But it's all good! The Lord has plans for you and nothing can stop the favor God has coming your way. He has blessings with your name on them that no one can reverse. So claim Fred's lyrics as your affirmation: *No weapon formed against me shall prosper, it won't work.* God's power will annihilate every fiery dart. Poof! Gone. It's been said, "The higher the level, the bigger the devil," but God is bigger than whatever opposes you. Words meant for evil, God will turn around for your good. He will bless you in the presence of your enemies.

HIGH NOTE:
No matter who's against you, God is always for you!

Tramaine HAWKINS

"Changed"

> Therefore, if anyone is in Christ, he is a new creation;
> old things have passed away; behold, all things have become new.

2 CORINTHIANS
5:17

Once you experience Jesus' love, you are never the same. The new birth experience changes your heart. The rest of you—your looks, your personality—remains uniquely you because that's how God fashioned you. Your heart—the inner you—is what the Lord works on.

You've probably met people who were transformed after receiving Christ as their personal Lord and Savior. Some folks have a more drastic conversion experience than others. Former drug dealers, substance abusers, prostitutes, and corrupt politicians may have a more sensational testimony than others because of the depth of their spiritual need, but all who experience the new creation in Christ can attest to this verse in Lady Hawkins' anointed song: *A change has come over me; He changed my life and now I'm free.*

Folks who have lived hard lives often gladly share how the Lord changed them. They make excellent evangelists and street preachers because they are not ashamed to tell people how God has made a difference in their broken lives. But everyone who accepts the love of Jesus is changed.

The Bible reveals that those who came into Jesus' presence were changed. Whether it was a word from Him, His healing touch, or even His gentle rebuke, they left His presence different. The Samaritan woman (John 4:9), Mary Magdalene (Mark 16:9), Zacchaeus (Luke 19:8), and of course Paul, who had the most dramatic conversion of all (Acts 9:15), are prime examples.

Once you experience Jesus' love, your life will never be the same.

HIGH NOTE:

Only the Lord can change a heart.

Tramaine Hawkins ♪ *"Changed"*

Israel HOUGHTON

"Love God, Love People"

" 'And you shall love the LORD your God with all your heart, with all your soul, with all your mind, and with all your strength.' This is the first commandment. And the second, like it, is this: 'You shall love your neighbor as yourself.' There is no other commandment greater than these."

MARK 12:30–31

Israel Houghton's upbeat song keeps Jesus' commandment simple: love God, love people. Loving God is easy for most of us. We can't see Him, but we know He exists through the Holy Spirit within us that testifies to Him. Loving people? Well, sometimes that's harder. Jesus knew we'd struggle in this area and gave many examples recorded in the Bible of sacrificial love toward others.

We meet people who are mean-spirited, spiteful, and narcissistic. Folks like these are hard to like, let alone love. But God wants us to love them. In the natural, this makes no sense at all. But the Lord loves them. And in His quest to make us more like His Son, He challenges us to go beyond the natural realm and tap into our spiritual sides by emulating Jesus' perfect example of love.

Jesus loved traitors (Judas). He loved those who sought to kill Him (the Pharisees). He loved undesirables (tax collectors). He loved until His last breath. Well, I'm not Jesus, you may say. He was sinless; we aren't. We will mess up. In certain situations, we will react very badly. Other times our egos will get in the way of love. We can't love sacrificially in our own strength. We must rely on the power of the Holy Spirit to help us love even when we don't want to. It's the only way to truly love others as Jesus did.

HIGH NOTE:
You can love people because of your love for God.

Israel Houghton ♪ *"Love God, Love People"*

57

Keith "Wonderboy" JOHNSON

"I Made It"

> Do you not know that those who run in a race all run,
> but one receives the prize?
> Run in such a way that you may obtain it.

Those of us who profess Christ know that even though we don't like tough times, they make us stronger. Just as Keith Johnson's lyrics confirm, *I never would have made it without You in my life*, all of us have gone through something that we wished we didn't have to experience.

An illness, death of a loved one, bankruptcy, or job loss can be painful, emotionally and physically. These hardships can extend for a long period of time. I have friends and family who've been out of work for years and were forced to liquidate their retirement accounts in order to survive. One of my sorority sisters lost both of her parents within weeks. Another friend has battled cancer off and on for years. The common denominator in all these examples was their dependence on God to see them through.

There's always a purpose for our pain. We can't see it at the time, but God doesn't make mistakes. He doesn't create our hardship but allows it because He's intentional about our growth. We may think that God is "punishing" us for some past sin, but that is not our loving God. (The devil will put all kinds of lies in your head.) Even in our pain, God arranges circumstances in our favor, providing solutions beyond the reach of human hands.

Stay focused on the Lord. You are destined to make it. Once the sun comes out, the birds start to chirp again, you will know that God brought you out. You will be grateful and relieved.

HIGH NOTE:
You get the lesson and God gets the glory because you made it.

Keith "Wonderboy" Johnson 𝄞 "I Made It"

59

Le'Andria JOHNSON

"Jesus"

> "And blessed is he who is not offended because of Me."
>
> MATTHEW 11:6

As much as I love books, I love movies more. In the early 1990s before Tyler Perry was on the scene, I pitched a Christian screenplay to Hollywood producers. I'd been warned that in Hollywood you could say "God" all you wanted, but never "Jesus." But I had written a Christian movie. Jesus was the centerpiece of my script. After a couple of years of brush-offs—some quite brash—I never tried again. Now, it's a new day! Not only is Jesus' name mentioned in movies and TV series, some have even been box office hits!

God's timing is always perfect. Matthew 24:14 says, "And this gospel of the kingdom will be preached in all the world as a witness to all the nations, and then the end will come." Biblical prophecy hinges on the gospel being preached all over the world. And there is no gospel without Jesus. He is the King of Kings and the Lord of Lords (Revelation 19:16). He is the Alpha and the Omega (Revelation 1:8). He is everything!

Let my Hollywood experience remind you that you may be negatively judged because of the Name that is above all names (Philippians 2:9). The criticism may be subtle or even harsh. However, Jesus clearly desires our allegiance to Him: "But whoever denies Me before men, him I will also deny before My Father who is in heaven" (Matthew 10:33).

HIGH NOTE:

Stand up for Jesus because He will always stand up for you.

Le'Andria Johnson & "Jesus"

Le'Andria Johnson & *"Jesus"*

Canton JONES

"Stay Saved"

But the fruit of the Spirit is
love, joy, peace, longsuffering, kindness,
goodness, faithfulness, gentleness, self-control.
Against such there is no law.

**GALATIANS
5:22–23**

Check out the video for this fun but truthful song. Canton Jones is shown in a succession of scenes where his patience is tested in situations we can all relate to. When you profess Christ and actually act Christlike, folks may ruffle your feathers. It's best to take the high road, but that's not to say you should be a pushover. Canton expresses it well: *Just because I'm Christlike doesn't mean I'm mice-like; I'm gonna be the bigger man.*

In challenging situations, state your case (in love) and keep it moving. Jesus said, "Agree with your adversary quickly" (Matthew 5:25). Petty arguments can rapidly escalate into full-blown fights. Many folks aren't alive today because they refused to walk away.

We always have a choice. When someone taunts me, I've found that if I refuse to engage them, they back off. My mom would say, "Never argue with a fool." Although I'm not confrontational by nature, when I've fallen into the devil's trap of going tit for tat, I've felt awful afterward. Not only did my behavior compromise my witness, I know the Lord wasn't pleased. That made me feel worse.

Stay prayed up. Realize it's spiritual warfare when people try to push your buttons or entice you into a confrontation. Know your Father is also watching. And it's Him we want to please.

HIGH NOTE:

Self-control is a fruit of the Spirit. Ask God for the strength to exercise it.

Canton Jones & *"Stay Saved"*

John P. KEE

"Blessings"

> And let us not grow weary while doing good,
> for in due season we shall reap if we do not lose heart.

GALATIANS
6:9

Most of our blessings are purely by God's grace and have nothing at all to do with our works. Other blessings, however, are indeed contingent upon what we do. The words *seed, planting, watering, harvest, reaping,* and *seasons* occur throughout Scripture. They illustrate multiplied consequences: when a seed is put in the ground, it will yield a bountiful harvest. Our actions play a role in determining our blessings.

Sowing and reaping is a vital principle in the kingdom of God, and the Bible contains many references to it. When you sow good seeds, you will reap a good harvest. It's the law of agriculture, and God uses it to show us that consequences to our actions are inevitable. Positive actions yield multiplied positive results. But as Galatians 6:9 reads, there's one condition: you can't give up. Like a patient farmer, you have to wait it out.

For most of us, waiting is the hardest part. We want to see our harvest right away. We must understand that God's timetable is not ours. He has no calendar or watch. He operates on His own schedule.

John P. Kee's lyrics *It's my harvest, I can count on it… They're coming y'all, blessings are coming!* remind you to continue to sow—love, kindness, time, money, whatever God leads you to do. Just sow, sow, sow! There's a blessing in giving (Acts 20:35), so it's a win for you regardless. But know this: you will reap your harvest, period. And at just the right time!

HIGH NOTE:

The good seeds you've sown will bring a harvest worth the wait!

John P. Kee 🎼 *"Blessings"*

65

Deon KIPPING

"I Don't Look Like (What I've Been Through)"

Deon Kipping ♪ "I Don't Look Like (What I've Been Through)"

> "When you pass through the waters, I will be with you;
> and through the rivers, they shall not overflow you.
> When you walk through the fire, you shall not be burned,
> nor shall the flame scorch you."

ISAIAH 43:2

This verse is so comforting. It's like getting a big hug from your dad after a bad day at school.

In the first part of the verse, it seems the Father is saying, "I know this issue is painful, but I'm with you every step of the way. Don't fret—Daddy's here." But the second part is the most reassuring: "Not only will this problem pass, there will be no evidence that there ever was a problem!"

Only God can be with you in the fire and assure you there will be no permanent damage or physical evidence that you'd been in a fire.

The Lord makes many promises throughout the Bible, but He doesn't promise us a pain-free life. We will have trouble (John 16:33). We grow through our hardships and disappointments, and just as important, God preserves us and holds us up as His showpieces for the world to see after we've come out on the other side.

So many of us are walking testimonies, having survived cancer, the death of children, domestic violence, and a myriad of seemingly unsurmountable odds. We've lived to tell the story. What could have crippled us, God used to empower us. Smiles replace tears. Joy replaces sadness. Victory replaces defeat. Thank God we don't look like what we went through!

HIGH NOTE:

Your victory in trials makes you God's showpiece.

Deon Kipping ♪ *"I Don't Look Like (What I've Been Through)"*

MARY MARY

"Go Get It"

The hand of the diligent will rule.

Proverbs 12:24

*T*he upbeat, motivating message *You were made to live a good life, and that's what I believe, so hit the floor, say a prayer, start working, you got to do something* couldn't be clearer: faith without works is dead (James 2:17).

Believing God's Word is easy. Dreaming is easy. But actually working toward your goals and dreams can be hard. But it is not impossible. No one gets blessed and God gets no glory from your unfulfilled dreams.

Are you one of those people who hate your job? Are you in a position that brings you no joy? What stops most people from making job changes is fear. Fear of failure. Fear of success. Fear of the unknown. But God has not given you a spirit of fear, but of power, and of love and a sound mind (2 Timothy 1:7). There's no limit to what God will do for you when you commit your dream to Him. He will open doors of opportunity, set you up with the right people, and provide resources—everything you need to succeed. So go get that blessing!

HIGH NOTE:
God wants you to go after your goals and dreams. It's your time!

Donnie McCLURKIN

"Stand"

Therefore take up the whole armor of God,
that you may be able to withstand in the evil day,
and having done all, to stand.

EPHESIANS 6:13

*N*o matter how many times I hear "Stand," one of my all-time favorite worship songs, something about it compels me to stop what I'm doing and lift my hands in praise and adoration to God. The song has an anointing upon it. The words *after you've done all you can, you just stand* bless me the most.

Most of us can testify that God has seen us through some pretty rough battles—sickness, loss of a loved one, financial ruin, divorce. So many challenges can beset us in a lifetime. We have prayed, cried, worried, and paced the floor when the pressure was on. I did all those things and more during my times of challenge. I'm one of those people who find it hard to just do nothing. But sometimes that's exactly what God wants us to do. Just stand.

Get quiet, get centered, and stay laser focused on God, not your problem. If you've indeed done everything in your human power to better your situation and you still haven't seen any results, you will, but in God's time. God may be perfecting patience in you. Your waiting is not in vain. Your breakthrough is on the way! Your change will come, and right on time. God's got this. And He's got you.

HIGH NOTE:

Trust that God is working all things together for your good . . . because He is!

Donnie McClurkin ♪ "Stand"

71

William McDOWELL

"I Give Myself Away"

Serve the LORD with gladness.

PSALM 100:2

*T*his beautiful worship song sums up the life of Christ—selflessness. *My life is not my own, to You I belong. I give myself, I give myself to You.* Jesus gave of Himself continually, despite how He may have felt. He pushed through fatigue, hunger, and frustration to minister to as many as possible. Their needs were great and He put them first. William McDowell's song expresses this same desire to serve God and others: *I give myself away so You can use me.* When we serve others, we serve God. How can we serve? Here are a few ideas:

Serve those less fortunate: Volunteer at a food pantry, women's shelter, or nursing home. Jesus said whatever you do for the disenfranchised you've done for Him (Matthew 25:40).

Serve in your church: The Lord said the harvest is plentiful but the laborers are few (Matthew 9:37). Whether you choose to usher, work in the nursery, or teach Sunday school, you can make a difference.

Serve your spouse: Marriage requires selflessness on many levels; it can be challenging. But there's nothing sweeter than seeing a couple try to "out-love" one another. A friend folds clothes for their family of eight while he watches Monday-night football. "It's one way I serve my wife," he beamed.

Serve your community: God commands us to love our neighbor as ourselves (Mark 12:31), so find ways to pitch in. Join a neighborhood watch or buy groceries for the dad who just lost his job.

HIGH NOTE:

Jesus is our perfect Example of selfless service.

William McDowell 𝄞 *"I Give Myself Away"*

VaShawn MITCHELL

"Nobody Greater"

> Therefore You are great, O Lord GOD.
> For there is none like You,
> nor is there any God besides You,
> according to all that we have heard with our ears.

2 SAMUEL 7:22

You can scour the earth in search of one greater than Jesus and you will come up empty. No one and nothing can replace Him. VaShawn's lyrics minister to our spirits with his personal affirmation: *I climbed up to the highest mountain, I looked all around, couldn't find nobody, way down into the deepest valley, looked all around down there, couldn't find nobody.*

The great God of all creation takes pleasure in helping His children. Nothing gets by Him. When we feel hopeless and desperate, we may turn to our family, our friends, our jobs, even our pastors for solace. Then, after we have exhausted all natural avenues, we turn to God. But He wants us to seek Him first, not as a last resort (Matthew 6:33).

The lyrics also attest to God's omnipotence: *awesome in all your ways and mighty is your hand.* God is on our side and will fight our battles. God is the Boss of all bosses, the Judge of all judges, and the Great Physician. There is nothing God can't do and no problem He can't solve. We can count on the Lord. There is simply nobody greater.

HIGH NOTE:
You can trust God with every aspect of your life. He is the great I Am!

VaShawn Mitchell 𝄞 *"Nobody Greater"*

J. MOSS

"Good & Bad"

> For I am persuaded that neither death nor life,
> nor angels nor principalities nor powers,
> nor things present nor things to come,
> nor height nor depth, nor any other created thing,
> shall be able to separate us from the love of God
> which is in Christ Jesus our Lord.

ROMANS 8:38–39

As much as we don't want to, we will disappoint God in some big or small way. We're human and imperfect; therefore, we will sin. Although we are forgiven by virtue of the blood of Jesus (1 John 1:7), we feel guilty and beat ourselves up. We equate God's unconditional love with our human love, which is almost always conditional. J. Moss' heartfelt song reminds us that God never turns His back on us: *You loved me through my good. You loved me through my bad. You didn't erase my future, because of my past. I'm glad you loved me through my good and my bad.*

(continued on next page)

J. Moss & *"Good & Bad"*

Although "bad" in Moss' song refers to our actions, it can also speak to the bad times in our lives, when we feel God couldn't possibly love us. This includes when we are "mad at God" or distant from the Lord after a major loss or disappointment. We stop going to church. We quit reading our Bible. We may even fall into sinful situations again. We all go through rebellious phases, especially when we are hurting. I did. After I'd lost my home to foreclosure, I stopped going to church. I couldn't even touch my Bible, let alone read it. I let the church members' calls go directly to voice mail. I didn't want to be bothered. I felt God had let me down. Just weeks before the foreclosure, I was in church every time the doors were open. You couldn't drag me out of there. I was hopeful God would miraculously save my piece of the American dream. He didn't.

I was a "baby" Christian back then. I thought God would shield me from bad things. I didn't know any better. It was my first major letdown. But even as I distanced myself from God and my church family, He loved me more than I knew. During my months-long temper tantrum, God never left my side. I know now that He never will, no matter whether times are good or bad.

God loves us in hard times and good times, when we are obedient and when we stray. He loves us always and forever. You can't run God off. He's with you through the good and the bad.

HIGH NOTE:
God's love for you will never change.

God's Love through Good and Bad

Memorize these verses that pertain to God's love for you in your particular situation, so you are always ready to speak that Scripture.

"For I know the thoughts that I think toward you,"
says the LORD,
"thoughts of peace and not of evil,
to give you a future and a hope."   JEREMIAH 29:11

"Yes, I have loved you with an everlasting love; therefore
with lovingkindness I have drawn you."   JEREMIAH 31:3

"But the very hairs of your head are all numbered. Do not
fear therefore; you are of more value than many sparrows."
          LUKE 12:7

"As the Father loved Me, I also have loved you; abide in
My love."   JOHN 15:9

In this the love of God was manifested toward us, that
God has sent His only begotten Son into the world, that we
might live through Him.   1 JOHN 4:9

William MURPHY

"You Reign"

> Say among the nations, "The LORD reigns;
> The world also is firmly established, it shall not be moved;
> He shall judge the peoples righteously."
>
> PSALM 96:10

*T*he day after the 2016 election, I saw a meme on Facebook that read, "No Matter Who Is President, Jesus Is King." The world watched as America became bitterly divided over the outcome of the election. Despondency, anger, fear, disillusionment, and even shock were the emotions displayed in the days and weeks that followed.

Undocumented workers feared deportation. Swastikas popped up near synagogues. Racial epithets were scrawled on school walls. Reports of hate crimes poured in from precincts around the country. America's citizens were up in arms—Christians included.

I, too, got caught up in the whirlwind of emotions and fear. Then God brought to my remembrance that HE is in total control. And I responded to God what William Murphy's lyrics state, *With power and majesty, dominion, authority You reign.*

No matter what, God is still on the throne of grace. Our Father has seen African Americans and other disenfranchised groups through the toughest of times and has never abandoned us. He will continue to watch over us as we fast, pray, and seek His face (2 Chronicles 7:14). We serve a God who sits high and looks low (Isaiah 40:22). Jesus, not an elected official, is the King of kings!

HIGH NOTE:
Regardless of our circumstances, our God reigns.

Jason NELSON

"Shifting the Atmosphere"

Let your light so shine before men,
that they may see your good works,
and glorify your Father in heaven.

MATTHEW
5:16

*H*ave you ever entered a room and you could immediately feel the tension from the people in it? Perhaps an argument or other unpleasant exchange had just taken place. You see it in their body language. You see it in their facial expressions. It makes you feel uncomfortable.

The Holy Spirit has given us the power to change our surroundings by shifting the atmosphere—of any situation.

Maybe your boss is having a bad day, but she breaks into a smile when you surprise her with a double latte. Your child gets a bad grade on a test he studied so hard for, but your love, confidence in him, and reassurance make him smile. You've had a major disagreement with your spouse, but you hug them tightly as they whisper, "I'm sorry," in your ear.

The atmosphere shifted when Jesus came on the scene. Jesus said we are the light of the world (Matthew 5:14) and we should let our light shine (v. 16). The love of Christ compels us to shine when light is needed. Sometimes a simple smile or the squeeze of our hand will change sadness to joy. Like Jesus, we have the power to shed light in dark places. Love enters a room and things change. You can be love, like Jesus was. We have the power in us to bring health, healing, and hope to those who have none.

HIGH NOTE:
Through our loving presence, we can shift the atmosphere in any setting.

Jason Nelson ❧ *"Shifting the Atmosphere"*

Charisse NELSON-McINTOSH

(with Richard Smallwood and Vision)

"Thank You"

> It is good to give thanks to the LORD,
> And to sing praises to Your name, O Most High.
>
>
> PSALM 92:1

I was taught to say "thank you" as soon as I could talk. My mother was a stickler; we had to be grateful. "Nobody has to do anything for you, so you'd better say thank you," she'd say. Whenever gifts were received, favors were granted, compliments were given, a "thank you" quickly followed. No one could ever accuse Ruthie's brood of being ungrateful. I passed on her wisdom to my own sons, who, when they were kids, would actually thank me for buying their favorite snacks!

On a human level, gratitude is a good virtue. But there's nothing anyone can do to match what God has done for us. We need to thank the One who not only created us, but created the entire universe. He likes to hear "thank you." Only one leper came back to thank Jesus after ten of them were healed. "So Jesus answered and said, 'Were there not ten cleansed? But where are the nine?'" (Luke 17:17).

How would you feel if you gave someone an expensive gift and they never said thank you? You'd think twice before doing that again. If that person gushed with grateful words, gave you a bear hug, plastered you with kisses, used your gift with obvious joy, and told everyone about it, you'd probably start saving for the next gift. Gratitude opens the door to greater blessings.

HIGH NOTE:
We can never say thank you enough for all the Lord has done for us.

Charisse Nelson-McIntosh ♪ *"Thank You"*

Smokie NORFUL

"I Need You Now"

The righteous cry out, and the LORD hears, and delivers them out of all their troubles.

PSALM 34:17

*T*his song reminds me of the countless number of times that I've seen posts from my Facebook friends who put out the urgent request for all "prayer warriors" to intercede, either for themselves or for a loved one.

Like the Israelites in Exodus 14:10, these friends know that when you are in dire need of God's help, you must cry out to Him. And have others cry out with you. I can relate to Smokie Norful's impassioned plea: *At this moment with my arms outstretched I need you to make a way.* When a newborn is given only a few hours to live, you cry out to God. When a car crash victim is rushed in for emergency surgery, you cry out to God. God is only a prayer away (Psalm 34:15). In crises, we have to put in a 911 call to the Lord and wait for His deliverance. He will come to our rescue.

Nobody knew that more than Moses. In Exodus 14, he and the children of Israel were chased by Pharaoh and his army after they fled Egypt. Terrified, they faced the Red Sea. The outlook was bleak for God's chosen people. Despite this terrifying scene, God had promised Moses they would cross that sea, and God kept His promise, as He always does. You know how the story ends!

HIGH NOTE:

Cry out to God in your time of need and see the salvation of the Lord!

Kelly PRICE

"Healing"

"For I am the LORD who heals you."

EXODUS 15:26

*I*t's been said that time heals all wounds. Not in every case. As time passes, the pain of some incidents will lessen. But there are traumatic events that only Jesus—not time—can heal. Since we are triune beings—mind, body, and spirit—we can be perfectly fine in one or two of those areas yet suffer in another one. Sexual assault, domestic violence, and abuse are childhood traumas that can still haunt us as adults. Children can't process pain the way adults can, and many simply bury it as if it never happened.

Deep childhood wounds need to be exposed in order to heal or they just "hide" inside us, wreaking havoc on the other areas of our lives. We carry the pain for years or even a lifetime. The Lord cares about troubled minds and broken spirits. While Jesus healed many physical ailments, He also healed those with emotional issues as well. The Samaritan woman couldn't keep a man (John 4:18). Mary Magdalene suffered from tormenting spirits (Luke 8:2). Physically they were fine, probably beautiful women, but they were very broken emotionally and mentally until they encountered Jesus. The disciple Thomas had trust issues, which he later overcame with Jesus' help (John 20:27–28).

You aren't alone and you don't have to suffer any longer. You can trust the Lord with your hurts and painful past. He wants to heal you from the inside out. Commit yourself to the process no matter how long it takes.

HIGH NOTE:
The Lord is invested in your emotional healing. You can trust Him.

Kelly Price & "Healing"

Hart RAMSEY

(with the NCC Family Choir)

"God's Up to Something Good"

> "'You *need* not fight in this *battle*; take your positions, stand and witness the salvation of the LORD who is with you, O Judah and Jerusalem. Do not fear or be dismayed; tomorrow go out against them, for the LORD is with you.'"

2 CHRONICLES
20:17 (AMP)

My good friend Denise Brown-Henderson hipped me to Pastor Hart Ramsey a few years ago when I was going through a rough patch. I signed up for his text message ministry, and his short, powerful daily messages still give me food for thought to this day.

His song is a reminder that God is always working things out for our good. It may take weeks, months, and yes, even years, but believe that what He's working on for you is major. I've learned in my Christian walk that God operates in His own time. He doesn't count time as we do (2 Peter 3:8). We can beg, plead, stomp our feet, cry, and sometimes even cuss (then repent!). Our temper tantrums don't move God. But our faith does.

I don't like waiting, but I know it's for my own good. There's a meme on Facebook that I absolutely love. A little girl is looking intently at Jesus with a small teddy bear in her hands. Jesus is kneeling in front of her, but He has a huge teddy bear behind his back. Jesus is telling her, "Trust me. I have something better."

From time to time, I look at that little cartoon to remind me that what God has for us is always bigger and better than anything we can ask, wish, or hope for. The chorus in this song tells it all: *You can have peace in the middle of the storm when you know joy is coming in the morning time.*

HIGH NOTE:

God is always up to something good wherever you are concerned.

Hart Ramsey 𝄞 *"God's Up to Something Good"*

Marvin SAPP

"I Win"

> Rejoice in the Lord always.
> Again I will say, rejoice!
>
> PHILIPPIANS 4:4

*Y*ou're a winner! You are stronger than you think. I'm sure you can relate to the first line: *I've had my share of tears, times when I wanted to give in.* Just when you think that life couldn't get any more painful and you don't know how you are going to make it, God in His infinite mercy and grace gives you supernatural strength to endure the trial or test you are facing. He is your Strong Tower. You win!

God is working on your behalf, even when it doesn't look like it. Bishop Sapp sings, *Out of your obstacles, God's working miracles.* Know that God works best behind the scenes. He's not a sportscaster; He's not going to give you play-by-play details of your deliverance. You have to trust Him. God doesn't take naps (Psalm 121:4). He's always up and moving things in your favor. You win!

God is bigger than your problem. It's hard not to look at the mess you're in while you're in it: overdue bills, health issues, marital woes—the list is endless. We live in a broken world and messes are unavoidable. But God doesn't want us to focus on the mess. He wants you to focus on Him. The mess is temporary. His love for you is eternal. You win!

HIGH NOTE:
With Jesus, you are an overcomer. You win!

Marvin Sapp ♪ *"I Win"*

Karen CLARK SHEARD

"Balm in Gilead"

But He was wounded for our transgressions,
He was bruised for our iniquities;
the chastisement for our peace was upon Him;
and by His stripes we are healed.

ISAIAH 53:5

When I first heard "Balm in Gilead," Karen Clark Sheard sang it with her siblings, the Clark Sisters, as a group. It was the late 1980s and I played it often in my car's cassette player. (Yes, it was *that* long ago!) The song's healing and reassuring words gave solace to many of us, all those years ago, and its message is just as appropriate today: *I know One who cares, found in Him peace of mind. I know One who's there, found a Friend so lovely and kind…*

"Balm" is soothing and brings instant relief—like a cooling ointment on a fresh scrape. Jesus is our Balm. People are hurting—in their minds, bodies, and spirits. Some suffer from mental illness. Some are spiritually empty. Some are physically ill. They need a comforting word, a reassuring presence, and most of all, hope. They need Jesus.

During His earthly ministry, Jesus took a holistic approach—He healed bodies (Matthew 4:24; Luke 4:40), He healed tormented minds (Matthew 8:16), and He healed those who had almost lost hope (Luke 8:43). He met people at the point of their need. And He will meet you at the point of yours.

HIGH NOTE:
"I am the Lord who heals you" (Exodus 15:26).

Karen Clark Sheard & *"Balm in Gilead"*

Kierra SHEARD

"Trumpets Blow"

> So the seven angels who had the seven trumpets prepared themselves to sound.

REVELATION 8:6

Few people will talk about the second coming of Christ. It's not exactly dinner conversation. Barring a few ministers who specialize in teaching end-time prophecy, not many pastors will touch it either. The book of Revelation is complex. As each day passes, we are getting closer and closer to Christ's return, but the only time eternity crosses our minds is when we think we're going to die. I had to chuckle at these lyrics Kierra Sheard sings: *Now you're praying, hoping for a bright light; if I make it, God, I swear I'm gonna act right.* How many of us have uttered that same desperate pseudoprayer when we got in a tight spot?

Before I came to Christ, I certainly did—and more than once. God knew those were just words. He knew I wasn't going to "act right," that I was going to do the same dumb thing again. But I thank God for His mercy and grace.

As biblical prophecy unfolds before our very eyes, the times will get tougher. We will have to fast and pray. We will need to stay rooted and grounded in the Word of God. Satan will take a mightier stand against believers and will try to deceive even the strongest Christians (Matthew 24:24), pulling out all the stops, knowing his time is coming to an end. God's calling us to be ready, as the final lines of the song proclaim: *Better get right, God's on your side; just be ready when the trumpet blows.*

HIGH NOTE:

God wants us to be ready in and out of season.

Richard SMALLWOOD

"Total Praise"

I will bless the LORD at all times;
His praise shall continually be in my mouth.

PSALM 34:1

When I hear good news or a powerful testimony, I can't help but say, "Praise the Lord!" It may seem cliché among church folk, but it's natural to give God the honor, glory, and praise that's due His name. "Total Praise" is a powerful worship song because it praises our awesome God. In a *Washington Post* interview, Richard Smallwood recalls a low point in his life and he says, "I was trying to write a pity-party song, but God pulled me to do a praise song. God said, 'I want your praise no matter what the situation you are in, good or bad.' It's about trusting him."

I couldn't agree more. Despite our circumstances, there is always something to praise God for. If God never does another thing for us, He's definitely worthy of our praise and adoration, so get your praise on!

HIGH NOTE:
God inhabits our praises . . . He is the great I Am!

Richard Smallwood ♪ *"Total Praise"*

Some Reasons to Praise God

There are countless reasons to praise God, but here are a few:

Praise Him for His mercy:

Praise the LORD! Oh, give thanks to the LORD, for He is good! For His mercy endures forever. PSALM 106:1

Praise Him for deliverance from enemies:

Sing to the LORD! Praise the LORD! For He has delivered the life of the poor from the hand of evildoers.

JEREMIAH 20:13

Praise Him for His holiness:

Exalt the LORD our God, and worship at His footstool—He is holy. PSALM 99:5

Praise Him because you are alive:

Let everything that has breath praise the LORD. Praise the LORD! PSALM 150:6

Micah STAMPLEY

"Our God"

The LORD lives! Blessed be my Rock!
Let the God of my salvation be exalted.

PSALM 18:46

My Redeemer lives! I don't know about you, but I'm so glad about that. When I first came to Christ, I read the Gospels voraciously. The book of John is still my favorite because it goes into so much detail on Jesus' time on earth. Micah Stampley's song is a testament to a Savior who sits high and looks low; a Redeemer who always has our best interests at heart; a loyal Son who petitions the Father on our behalf.

Father God is Spirit (John 4:24) and never had a human body, so He has not experienced aches and pains, exhaustion, emotional distress, or hunger. But His only begotten Son has. We know from the Gospels that Jesus' earthly life was no walk in the park. We see Jesus hungry, angry, tired, betrayed, insulted, and frustrated. What better Savior to have than one who knows what human weakness feels like? Jesus has been there. He knows what we're going through. He knows what we need. We don't have a passive savior or a man-made god. We have a Savior who has felt what we feel, experienced what we experience (Hebrews 4:15). Our God is alive and well, sitting on the throne of grace at the right hand of the Father.

Our God desires relationship, not religion, and love, not hate and condemnation. He wants all of us because He gave all of Himself to us. The words of Micah Stampley's great song testify to that: *Our God is greater, our God is stronger, Lord, you are higher than any other.* Aren't you glad that He is?

HIGH NOTE:
Our God reigns in heaven and on the earth.

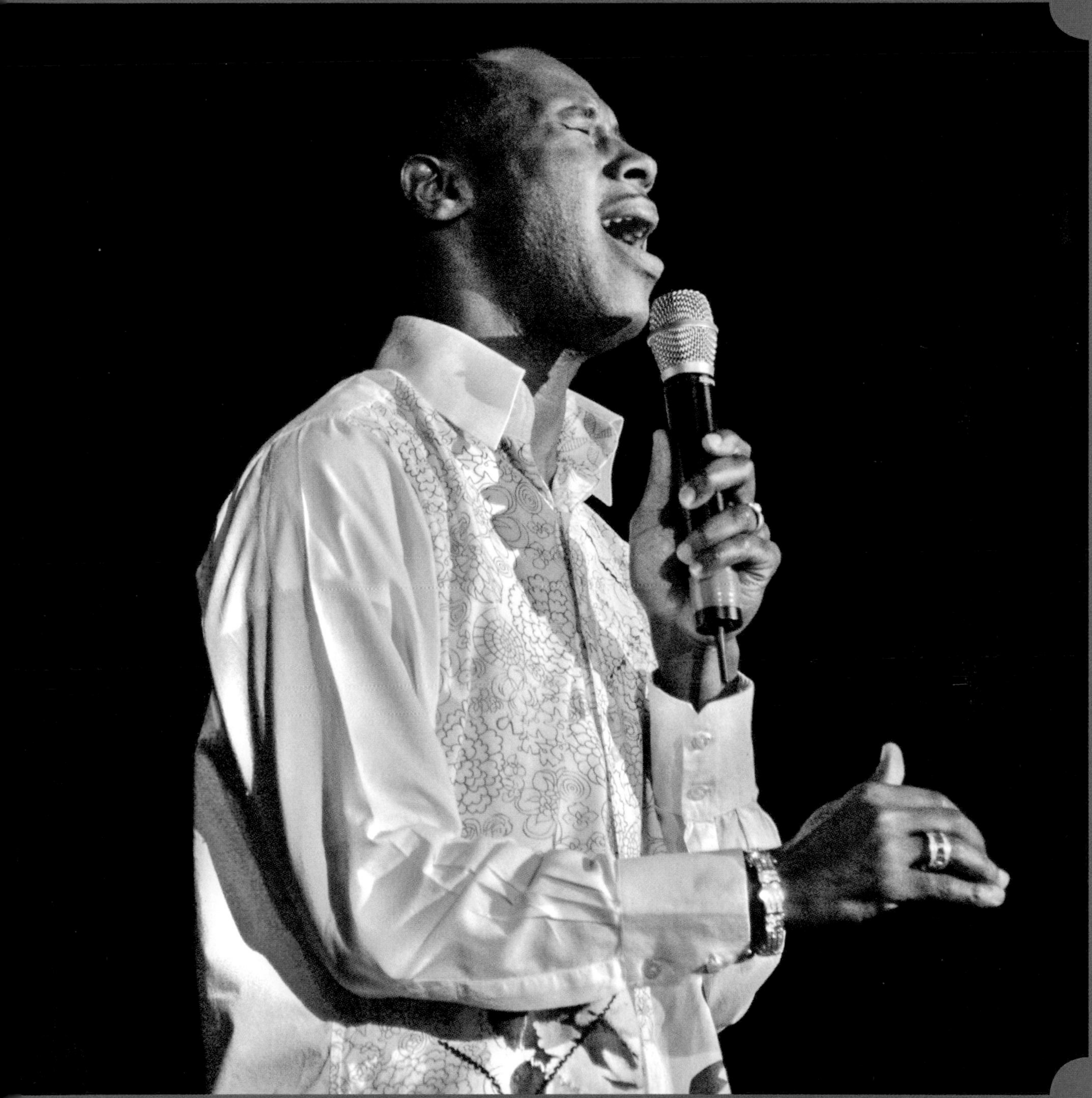

Micah Stampley 𝄞 *"Our God"*

Kathy TAYLOR

"Oh, How Precious"

> How precious is Your lovingkindness, O God! Therefore the children of men put their trust under the shadow of Your wings.
>
> PSALM 36:7

*T*he Lord's name is indeed precious. Psalm 8:1 reads, "O LORD, our Lord, how excellent is Your name in all the earth." But our relationship with Him is also precious.

Some good folks are sitting in church every Sunday, listening to the Word of God, singing along with the choir about the goodness of Jesus, and they have no personal relationship with Him. You may have been baptized as a child, and now that you're an adult, you go to church because that's what you've done all your life. You know church but you don't know God. I love Joyce Meyer's take on it: "Just because you go to church doesn't mean you're a Christian. I can go sit in the garage all day and it doesn't make me a car."

Scripture admonishes us to assemble together (Hebrews 10:25). We are stronger together, and there's nothing like lifting our voices to God in corporate praise. God loves it. But at the end of the day, each one of us will face Christ for ourselves. "For we must all appear before the judgment seat of Christ, that each one may receive the things done in the body, according to what he has done, whether good or bad" (2 Corinthians 5:10).

Scripture says that if you confess that you are a sinner, believe that Jesus Christ paid the penalty for your sin, and repent, you will be saved (Romans 3:23–24). It's imperative that we cultivate a loving, trusting relationship with the Lord here on earth, because when we get to heaven, we want Him to recognize us!

HIGH NOTE:

People will fail you—constantly. Jesus will never fail you.

Kathy Taylor & *"Oh, How Precious"*

Tonéx

"Make Me Over"

> But now, O Lord, You are our Father; we are the clay, and You our potter; and all we are the work of Your hand.
>
> Isaiah 64:8

In Romans 7:15, Paul said, "For I do not understand my own actions [I am baffled and bewildered by them]. I do not practice what I want to do, but I am doing the very thing I hate [and yielding to my human nature, my worldliness—my sinful capacity]" (AMP). We've all been in Paul's shoes and may still struggle with certain issues. For example, we want to tithe but don't. We don't want to tell a lie, but we do. The line in Tonéx's song, *You know my other side, I can no longer hide*, reminds us that God knows our weaknesses and shortcomings and loves us despite them, but He wants us to do better.

Most of us still struggle with things we thought for sure we'd be done with once we became born again: bad tempers, fornication, lying, jealousy, procrastination, swearing—you name it. Although our spirits have been reborn and we are new creations in Christ (2 Corinthians 5:17), we will constantly need forgiveness and redemption because as long as we are in these earthly bodies, we will wrestle with something. The Holy Spirit is your Helper, so ask Him to help you with problem areas. He will guide you through the rough spots.

You've heard the saying, "Please be patient with me; God is not through with me yet," and He really isn't. We are perpetual works in progress. God, the Master Potter, is at the wheel, shaping, cutting, smoothing, and molding us into who He wants us to be. God is "making us over" to be more like His Son.

HIGH NOTE:

God is molding you into who He created you to be. Be patient with yourself.

Tye TRIBBETT

"If He Did It Before... Same God"

Jesus Christ is the same yesterday, today, and forever.

HEBREWS 13:8

Some songs are so upbeat and empowering, they could be anthems. This is one of them.

One of the Lord's greatest gifts to us is our ability to remember. We remember songs from years gone by. We remember key life events, like when we got married or had a child. We remember our loved ones who have passed on. But when we get in a crisis, sometimes we forget how God has delivered us in the past. This song reminds us.

Please be, encouraged, this is not the first storm you've been through. You've been through worse, you didn't come this far just to lose. These are my favorite lines in the song. If you've lived long enough, you probably have been through worse. But you will need the Lord's help again. Your back will be against the wall—again. This time it may actually be worse; this might be a bigger giant than the last time. This could be a bloody battle, not a fistfight. Maybe there's no quick fix or easy solution. This one could require prayer and fasting. But the song confirms, *Same God right now, same God back then.* "For I am the LORD, I do not change; therefore you are not consumed, O sons of Jacob" (Malachi 3:6).

We can't figure God out, and He may not deliver us in the same way as last time, but I know one thing: He is the Originator of the repeat performance!

HIGH NOTE:

If God delivered you before, He will do it again.

Trin-i-tee 5:7

"God's Grace"

> For by grace you have been saved through faith,
> and that not of yourselves; it is the gift of God.
>
>
> EPHESIANS 2:8

*P*icture this: You're driving one beautiful sunny day. Then, out of nowhere, a distracted driver swerves into your lane, just barely avoiding a head-on collision. Your eyes widen in shock at the near fatal accident. "Thank you, Jesus," you mutter. The words of this song suddenly ring true: *It's by God's grace, all things through Christ Jesus. No weapon formed against me shall prosper.*

Or you're standing in line at your favorite department store, waiting to pay for your item. Even though it's on sale, it's still pricey. You know it's a splurge, but you've saved up for it. The lady behind you taps you on the shoulder and whispers, "Miss, I have an extra VIP coupon—forty percent off. Today's the last day you can use it." She smiles and presses it into your hand. You express your gratitude to her and smile. "Thank you, Jesus."

Whether it's a close call or a God-sent coupon, God looks out for His children. "Grace" by definition means "unmerited favor." You can't earn God's favor, and He gives it to us whether we are "good" or not. That's the grace that is truly amazing!

HIGH NOTE:
God's grace is always more than enough.

Uncle REECE

"Until I Pass Out"

Then David danced before the LORD with all his might.

2 SAMUEL 6:14

How do you get your praise on? Do you sing? Shout hallelujah? Dance? Or silently lift your hands in quiet worship? Praise is such an individual thing that there is no right or wrong way to do it as long as it's from a pure and sincere heart.

Miriam danced and even played the tambourine when she saw Pharaoh and his army swallowed up in the Red Sea (Exodus 15:20). And of course we know King David danced before God with reckless abandon—and he didn't care who was watching either! Throughout the Bible, there are verses about praising God with dance, timbrel, and harp (Psalm 149:3) and even stringed instruments and flutes (Psalm 150:4).

I remember when Kirk Franklin came on the scene. His lively and Spirit-filled songs reached a younger audience who loved God but also loved contemporary music. And yes, they were danceable! He opened the door for young ministers like Uncle Reece, who sings, *And please don't be alarmed if when the music comes on I begin to dance and run across the room until I can barely catch my breath.* Whether you're like Uncle Reece or are a quiet praiser, God is waiting for you to show Him some love with your praise.

HIGH NOTE:
God is worthy of your praise—however you choose to do it.

Hezekiah WALKER
"I Need You to Survive"

For where two or three are gathered together in My name, I am there in the midst of them.

MATTHEW
18:20

The lyrics of Bishop Hezekiah's song are short, powerful, and true: *I need you, you need me. We're all a part of God's Body.* God loves fellowship among His children. It's always been God's plan for us to love and serve one another. The Christian walk was never meant to be a solitary one. Constant and sustained fellowship with positive, uplifting believers is a surefire way to remain accountable to God.

Two of my dearest friends, Tyshaun and Marlene, saw me through some of my darkest hours. I didn't have a church home at the time and my attendance was spotty. These sisters *were my church*. They prayed for me. They fasted with me and held me up when my knees buckled under the pressure. I had no doubt that God had placed them in my life. As the song attests, *it is His will that every need be supplied. You are important to me. I need you to survive.* I needed Christian fellowship and He provided it. God knew I didn't have the strength to seek it out on my own, so He hand delivered those two blessings.

Is there a "lone saint" in your church? Ask the Holy Spirit how you can disciple the person. A warm smile or hug may be all the encouragement that's needed to show you care. We are each other's keepers!

HIGH NOTE:

We are never alone!

THE WALLS GROUP

"Great Is Your Love"

> Nor height, nor depth, nor any other created thing, shall be able to separate us from the love of God which is in Christ Jesus our Lord.
>
> ROMANS 8:39

God taught me a good lesson one day in the produce section of the supermarket. I picked up a Fuji apple. It looked perfect. I spotted a bruise. I tossed it back. Picked up another. Oh no—a gash. Flipped it back on the mound. Fifteen minutes later, I finally had about seven apples in my plastic bag. Why so long? I wanted the perfect apple. I did not want fruit that was bruised or cut or had been a feast for bugs. Then the Holy Spirit ministered to me. God's love for us is so great, He takes us just as we are—imperfections and all.

How many times have you messed up and thought God couldn't possibly love you? Can you imagine how we'd look if we had a spot or blemish for every time we sinned? We'd probably want to stay indoors for the rest of our lives. I know I would!

When we sin, God doesn't toss us away because of our imperfection. He picks us up, dusts us off, and gently lets us know we are loved. End of story. His love for us is greater than we could ever imagine. Jeremiah 31:3 reminds us, "The LORD has appeared of old to me, saying: 'Yes, I have loved you with an everlasting love.'"

HIGH NOTE:
No matter what you do, God's love for you will never change.

Melvin WILLIAMS

"Cooling Water"

> Repent therefore and be converted, that your sins may be blotted out, so that times of refreshing may come from the presence of the Lord.

ACTS 3:19

*T*his lively song reminds me of the few summers spent on my grandmother's porch in South Carolina. My mom always loved upbeat gospel songs, and "Cooling Water" would have been right up her alley. I'm sure she's snapping her fingers in heaven right now!

God's Word is refreshing like water, and the Bible often makes references to water. If you've ever had a tall glass of water on a scorching, hot day, you know how satisfying it is. Soda, ice tea, milk, or even flavored waters can't take the place of good, old-fashioned H_2O. Your fellowship with the Lord is similar—there just is no substitute. Those who try to replace God with material things always walk away empty. What good is sporting your Gucci bag if you don't have peace? You can tool around in your Benz (with your fair-weather friends snuggled in the backseat) and have no joy. God will grant us the desires of our heart (Psalm 37:4)—Gucci bags and Benzes included—especially if we worked hard to attain them, but He won't be replaced by them. Melvin Williams sings, *Sleepless nights and so much pain. I couldn't see no sunshine, nothing but rain.* That sounds like someone in desperate need of a Savior.

When you're hurting, it doesn't matter if you're sleeping on a cot or a three-thousand-dollar mattress, pain is pain. But a life with Christ makes all the difference. You will have peace through the discomfort. The chorus sings, *When He raised me…it felt just like cooling water.* He is our Living Water (John 4:10) and promises us that we'll never thirst again for anything else.

HIGH NOTE:

Nothing satisfies like Christ—our Living Water.

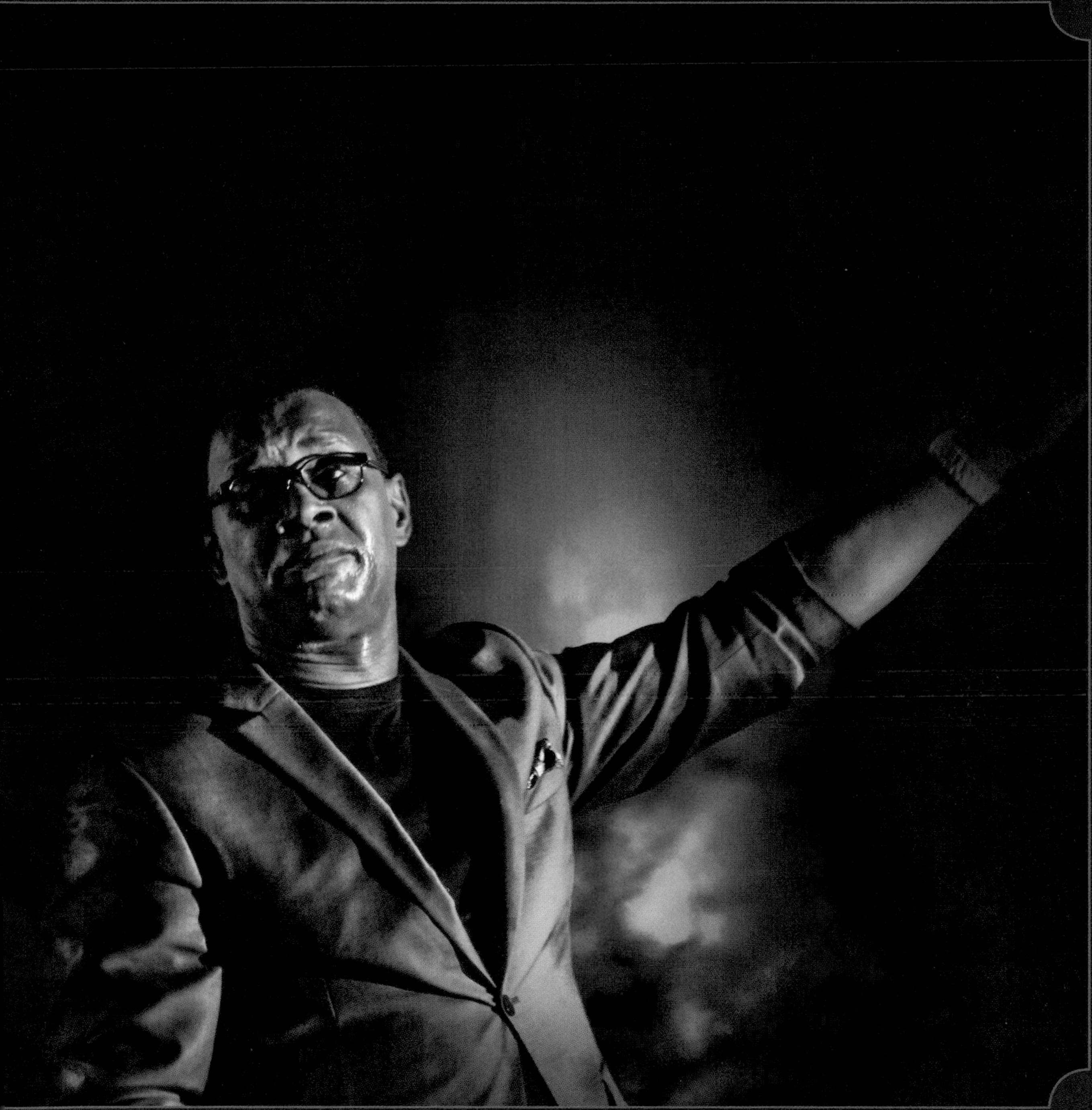

Melvin Williams 𝄞 "Cooling Water"

Michelle WILLIAMS

"If We Had Your Eyes"

But the LORD said to Samuel, "Do not look at his appearance or at his physical stature, because I have refused him. For the LORD does not see as man sees; for man looks at the outward appearance, but the LORD looks at the heart."

1 SAMUEL 16:7

Try as we might, it's hard not to judge others: how they look, what they're driving, their level of education. The list goes on. It's human nature to want to feel we're better, smarter, prettier, more whatever than the next person. Even when it comes to sin, we judge "their sin" as worse than "our sin." To make ourselves look bigger and others smaller is ungodly, an insecurity rooted in pride. Worse, it's a setup for disaster (Proverbs 16:18) and God hates it. The chorus of Michelle Williams' powerful song is so true. *People judge from what they see, but Lord you see the heart*. Thank God that He doesn't see us the way we see others.

The people we "write off" are the very ones God will use for His glory. The characters Jesus encountered in His earthly ministry were far from perfect. To us, Peter was an impulsive hothead. To Jesus, he was a warrior of the faith. He even referred to him as a "rock" and foundation for His church (Matthew 16:18). To us, Mary Magdalene was a lost and wayward woman. To Jesus, she was a precious daughter and faithful servant—the first one to see Him after His resurrection. We see flaws; He sees potential.

Pray for God to give you His eyes so you can see others as He sees them—with love.

HIGH NOTE:
Choose to see people as God sees them and as He sees you.

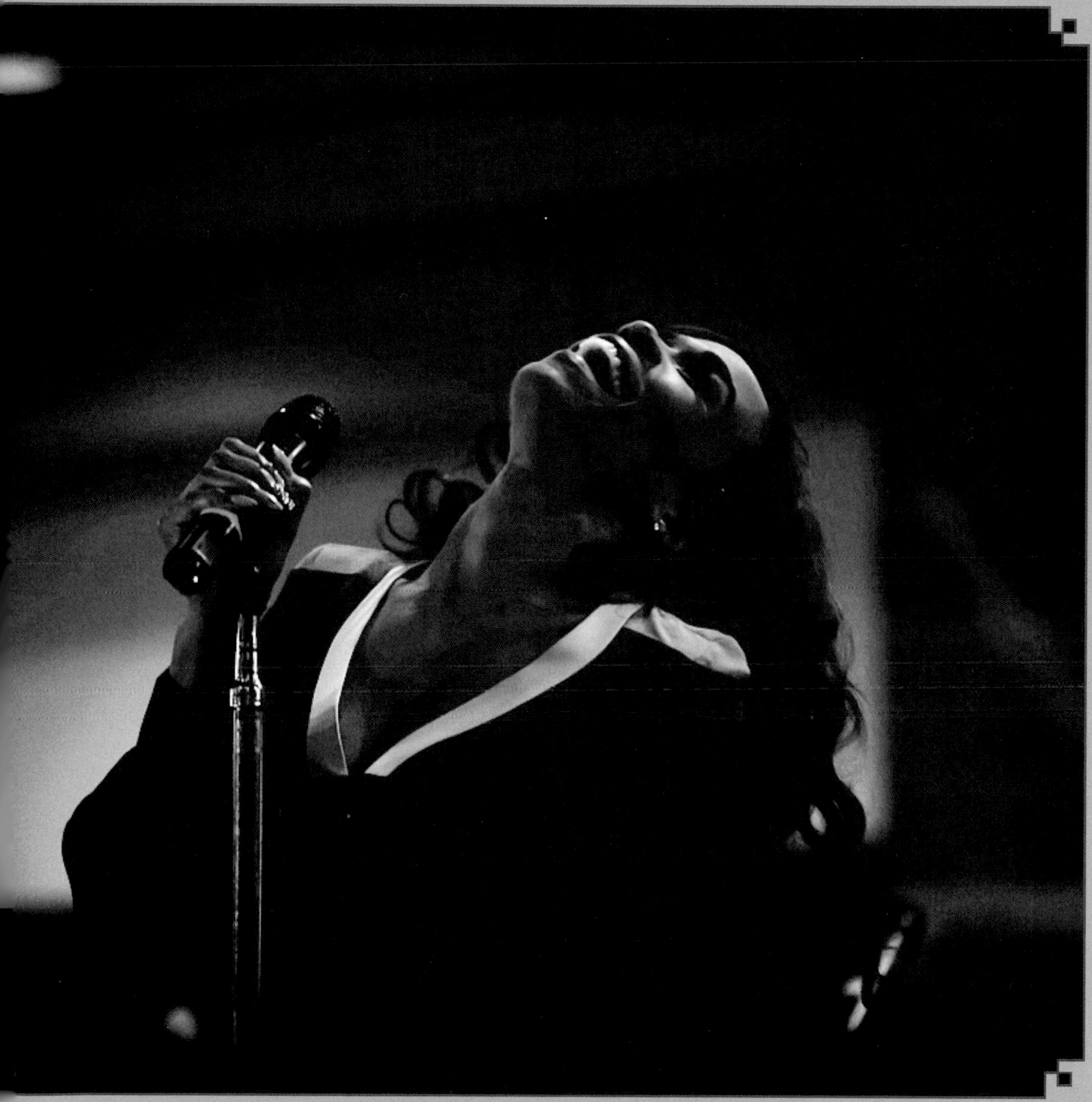

BeBe WINANS

"In Harm's Way"

> Greater love has no one than this,
> than to lay down one's life for his friends.

JOHN 15:13

*I*n some occupations, workers willingly put themselves in harm's way. Soldiers, law enforcement, and firefighters immediately come to mind, but bomb squad members, Secret Service agents, hazmat workers, and many others do, too. Due to the risky nature of their jobs, their lives hang in the balance every time they leave for work. Civil rights leaders such as Rev. Dr. Martin Luther King Jr., Medgar Evers, and Malcolm X put their lives on the line for the cause of freedom and equality for all. They proved their loyalty until their last breath. We owe a debt of gratitude to these brave Americans and our slain leaders for their duty, sacrifice, and service.

Yet, as noble as they all are, they have no eternal home for us. But Jesus does. BeBe Winans sings, *Because of love you placed yourself in harm's way*, and indeed He did. From being pursued by Herod at birth to his crucifixion, Jesus was always a moving target. However, Jesus still went where He knew He would face hostility. Preaching the gospel and healing those who needed it were more important to Him than avoiding the religious "haters." He endured their insults, sarcasm, ridicule, and finally, the beatings whose bloody trail followed Him to the cross. He was on a mission from God and nothing was going to stop God's Master Plan for humankind. Christ's love for us allowed Him to willingly lay down His life and present Himself a living, sinless sacrifice. The song testifies, *The price you paid, I could never repay.* Truer words were never spoken.

HIGH NOTE:
There's no greater sacrifice than the one made by Jesus.

BeBe Winans & *"In Harm's Way"*

123

CeCe WINANS
"Alabaster Box"

And behold, a woman in the city who was a sinner, when she knew that Jesus sat at the table in the Pharisee's house, brought an alabaster flask of fragrant oil, and stood at His feet behind Him weeping; and she began to wash His feet with her tears, and wiped them with the hair of her head; and she kissed His feet and anointed them with the fragrant oil.

LUKE 7:37–38

Three Scripture references relate the story of the woman who anointed Jesus with costly oil from an alabaster flask (Luke 7:37–38, Matthew 26:7, and Mark 14:3), but the one that strikes me the most is the account from Luke because Jesus confronts and silences the Pharisee who criticized this "sinful woman" for her public display (vv. 44–46). Jesus saw it as an act of love and gratitude. The Pharisee saw it as a waste. He didn't respect Jesus enough to pay homage to Him in the smallest of ways, let alone revere Him and bring Him a sacrificial gift. Dejected and probably dismissed as a prostitute, the woman recognized and valued the love Jesus showed her. She loved Jesus with all her heart, so she not only gifted Him with the oil, she gifted Him with her own broken spirit. That flask of perfume was expensive. But what He gave her was priceless: unconditional love, forgiveness, and acceptance.

Anyone who's experienced Christ's love can relate to the lyrics as CeCe Winans sings, *You did not feel what I felt when He wrapped His love all around me, and you don't know the cost of the oil in my alabaster box.* He meets us at the point of our need, just as He did for this woman. Jesus wants and deserves all of us. What are you holding on to that will be hard to let go of? The Lord wants you to surrender it all to Him.

HIGH NOTE: The gift of Christ's love is priceless.

CeCe Winans ♭ *"Alabaster Box"*

Marvin WINANS

"I'm Over It Now"

He heals the brokenhearted
and binds up their wounds.

PSALM 147:3

*S*he died of a broken heart" may sound tragically romantic, but there's no pain like heartbreak. When you've been betrayed, rejected, neglected, or abused by the one you loved, it's not easy to bounce back. Whether it's a decades-long marriage or short-lived courtship, matters of the heart hurt.

Anniversaries, your favorite restaurant, birthday gifts, and other memories of the love you shared can cause sleepless nights, crying spells, and depression. As Marvin Winans' lyrics state, *And every night I'd pray, Lord, let this cup pass.* You just want it to be over. But healing is a process and can't be rushed. The Lord knows this and wants to heal your heart so that you don't become bitter or angry. You will get to a place where you can say, "I'm over it now," as the song states, so be patient with yourself as you heal.

Pray and ask God to mend your broken heart.

Forgive the other person and forgive yourself (you're only human—and so are they). This may take time, but just commit to do it.

Get support from your pastor, counselor, or therapist.

Heal before you date again. You're vulnerable and the devil knows it. Don't give him a foothold.

Savor your "alone time" and use it to draw close to Jesus, who will never abandon you.

Love again. Ask God to send the person He has ordained just for you.

HIGH NOTE:
You deserve true love and you're worthy of it.

Marvin Winans ♪ *"I'm Over It Now"*

Vickie WINANS

"Shake Yourself Loose"

> Then Paul [simply] shook the creature off into the fire and suffered no ill effects.

ACTS 28:5 (AMP)

*T*he verse above illustrates how the power of God allows us to "shake off" those things that seek to harm us, distract us, deter us, and hinder us from living a victorious Christian life. It refers to an incident where a poisonous snake latched onto Paul's arm, but he was not harmed. The Amplified version of Acts 28:5 says he "simply" shook the snake off, like it was no big deal, a mere distraction. God wants us to see that even though we may be in a perilous situation, His power supersedes it.

I'm sure you can think of a situation that could have harmed (or killed) you, but it didn't. It was a close call, but God allowed you to "simply" shake it off. In this move-your-feet, empowering song, Vickie Winans encourages us to *shake loose everything that binds you up.* As Paul "simply" shook off that viper that could have killed him, we need to shake off things that can kill our spirit and our witness.

What do you have to shake off? If you are holding on to things that you know you need to eliminate, let them go. God will help.

HIGH NOTE:
God will help you shake free of anything that hinders your success.

Vickie Winans ♪ *"Shake Yourself Loose"*

129

Pray

Father God, Your Word says that Jesus came to set the captives free. You have given us the power over the enemy, so I break the strongholds that seek to hold me down, hold me up, and hold me hostage. I shake off all distractions, negative influences, bad habits, self-destructive behavior, and anything or anyone that attempts to stall Your plan for my life. Your Word says that he whom the Son has set free is free indeed, and I walk in that freedom now. Thank you for delivering me. In Jesus' name I pray. Amen.

Vickie Winans ♪ *"Shake Yourself Loose"*

Acknowledgments

To my Lord and Savior, Jesus Christ: There's no me without You. Words cannot describe how thankful I am to be Your disciple and, most of all, Your child. You brought me through the fire without even the faintest smell of smoke. So glad we're in this thing together.

To my sons, Jerry Jr. and David Mackey: You two were my rocks and my warriors. I'm so proud of the men you've both become. Thank you for your unconditional love and support. I don't care if you are grown men—you will always be my babies!

To my coauthor, B. Jeffrey Grant-Clark: Your friendship and prayers (and care packages!) got me through some mighty-hard days. I thank God for allowing us to merge our talents and use them for His glory.

To my awesome editor, Adrienne Ingrum: You are a godsend. Thank you for immediately catching my vision for this book. I'm so blessed to have such a smart and powerful woman of God in my corner.

To Denise Brown-Henderson: You introduced me to Jeff at you and Pastor Ray's wedding and we are eternally grateful. Thank you for allowing God to use you.

To my earth angels: Pat Lomax, Tyshaun Bishop, Marlene Robinson, Brigitte Weeks, Karl McNeill, Rhonda Hargrove, and Robert Butter. Thank you for being there when I needed you most and for being my village. Your friendship is priceless.

Many thanks to my family, friends, readers, reviewers, bloggers, radio hosts, churches, sorors of Delta Sigma Theta Sorority Inc., and so many others who supported my first baby, *Sistergirl Devotions: Keeping Jesus in the Mix on the Job.* You all were a blessing; your love won't ever be forgotten.

—*Carol*

First, thanQ to my three "kidults":

Dawn (Byron), thanQ for always making me think bigger.

Damone (Nadine)—DUDE! I couldn't have done this without your incredible graphic and retouching skills, the 2 a.m. text message updates, and your ever-cool demeanor when I was trippin'.

Melanie (Billy), thanks for keeping me humble with your "Yes, that's nice" responses when asked what you thought about the images...lol!

To PopPop's 4Ms—Madison, Morgan, Mia, McKenzie—and "HIM" Samuel Benjamin, thanQ.

To my family: the Clarks, Grants, and Harrises—thanQ for letting me practice on y'all all these years.

A special thanQ to Denise Brown-Henderson for taking the time on your wedding day to introduce me to Carol Hill-Mackey.

My friend and now coauthor, Carol M. Mackey, thanQ you for taking me under your wing, walking me through this process, and always keeping me and my family covered in prayer.

Kirk Franklin!!! Man, thanQ for such an amazing and heartfelt foreword...My dude for life!

Cheryl Brown-Marks, "my partner" 4 LIFE: thanQ for always having my back.

Neily Dickerson, you always said I should think about being a "fo' real, fo' real" photographer.

Thanks to my Verity / RCA Inspiration crew: Carla Williams, Tara Griggs-Magee, Jazzy Jordan, Jojo Pada, Kymberlee Norsworthy, Damon Williams, Tricia Newell, Jeremy Castro, Clyde Duffie, Tamar Poole-Rand, Eboni Funderburk, Monica Bacon, Vickie Mack Lataillade, Justin Tomlinson, Christopher Anderson, Christine Anderson, Mark Michel, Sammantha Lee Winston, Joseph Burney, Jackie Patillo, Tracey Artis, and Debra "Snoopy" Hanna—thanQ for always encouraging me.

Adrienne Ingrum, thanQ for allowing me to see a longtime dream come to pass, and thanQ to her able assistant, Grace Tweedy Johnson.

To my mentors, Kimberly Wilson-Mills and Yivelle McKinley—thanQ. "You 2 ladies took me under your wings and gave me the opportunity to learn from 2 of the most amazing photographers on the planet!"

Finally, I am grateful to God for giving me the opportunity to share these images with the world.

—B. Jeffrey

Recommended Listening

Yolanda Adams

Becoming

What a Wonderful Time

Day by Day

Yolanda Adams

Believe

The Experience

Christmas with Yolanda Adams

Mountain High... Valley Low

Songs from the Heart

Yolanda: Live in Washington

More than a Melody

Save the World

Through the Storm

Just as I Am

Shari Addison

Shari Addison

Crystal Aikin

Crystal Aikin

All I Need

Rance Allen

Closest Friend

The Live Experience

All the Way

Miracle Worker

You Make Me Wanna
Dance

Up above My Head

Phenomenon

Hear My Voice

I Give Myself to You

Ain't No Need of Crying

I Feel Like Going On

Smile

Truth Is Where It's At

Rance Allen Group

Brothers

Say My Friend

Vanessa Bell Armstrong

Timeless

The Experience

Walking Miracle

Sing to Glory

Brand New Day

Desire of My Heart

The Secret Is Out

Something on the Inside

Chosen

Wonderful One

The Truth about Christmas

Following Jesus

Vanessa Bell Armstrong

Peace Be Still

Amber Bullock

So in Love

Thank You

Kim Burrell

From a Different Place

The Love Album

No Ways Tired

Live in Concert

Everlasting Life

Try Me Again

Jonathan Butler

Free

Living My Dream

Merry Christmas to You

Grace and Mercy

Gospel Goes Classical

Faith Love & Joy: Great Spiritual
   Inspirations

So Strong

Live in South Africa

Gospel Days

Brand New Day

Jonathan

The Worship Project

Surrender

The Source

Story of Life

Do You Love Me?

Head to Head

Heal Our Land

7th Avenue

More than Friends

Jonathan Butler

Introducing Jonathan Butler

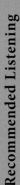

Myron Butler

On Purpose (with Levi Butler)

Worship

Double Take

Shirley Caesar

Fill This House

Good God

A City Called Heaven

Revisited

After 40 Years: Still Sweeping through the City

I Know the Truth

Live: Taking It Back to Gospel

Every Day Is Mothers Day

Be Careful of the Stones You Throw

Shirley Caesar and Friends

Feel the Spirit

From the Heart

Hymns

You Can Make It

I'll Go

Christmas with Shirley Caesar

Shirley Caesar & the Caravans

The Lord Will Make a Way

A Miracle in Harlem

Just a Word

Shirley Caesar Live...He Will Come

Don't Drive Your Mama Away

King and Queen of Gospel, Vol. 2 (with James Cleveland)

He Touched Me

Why Me Lord

Old Apple Tree

Throw Out the Lifeline

Christmasing

I Remember Mama

He's Working It Out for You

Celebration

Go

He Heard Me Cry

Live in Chicago with Rev. Milton Brunson and the Thompson Community Singers

Sailin'

Jesus, I Love Calling Your Name

Rejoice!

Shirley Caesar Sings Her Gospel Favorites, Vol. 2

First Lady

Go Take a Bath

My Testimony

Byron Cage

Memoirs of a Worshipper

Faithful to Believe

Live at the Apollo: The Proclamation

An Invitation to Worship
The Prince of Praise
Byron Cage
Transparent in Your Presence
Dwell Among Us

Erica Campbell

Help
Help 2.0

Kurt Carr

Bless This House
Just the Beginning
Come Let Us Worship
One Church
Awesome Wonder
No One Else
Serious about It!
Together

Jacky Clark-Chisholm

Expectancy
Oil of God

Dorinda Clark-Cole

Dorinda Clark-Cole
The Rose of Gospel
Take It Back
I Survived
In the Face of Change
Living It

Tasha Cobbs

Grace
One Place Live

Joann Rosario Condrey

Joyous Salvation
Now More Than Ever...Worship
More, More, More

Y'Anna Crawley

The Promise

Andraé Crouch

Live in Los Angeles
The Journey
Just Andraé
Mighty Wind
Take the Message Everywhere
Soulfully
He's Everywhere
Kings of Gospel (with Walter Hawkins)
The Gift of Christmas
Pray
Mercy
Let's Worship Him
Finally
No Time to Lose
Don't Give Up
Autograph
I'll Be Thinking of You
Live in London
Andraé Crouch & the Disciples
This Is Another Day
Take Me Back
Keep on Singin'
I Don't Know Why Jesus Loved Me
Live at Carnegie Hall

Kirk Franklin

Losing My Religion
Hello Fear
The Fight of My Life
Hero
The Rebirth of Kirk Franklin
Kirk Franklin Presents 1NC
The Nu Nation Project
God's Property
Whatcha Lookin' 4
Christmas

Travis Greene

The Hill
Stretching Out
The More

Deitrick Haddon

Masterpiece
Deitrick Haddon's LXW (League of Xtraordinary Worshippers)
R.E.D. (Restoring Everything Damaged)
A Beautiful Soul
Church on the Moon
Revealed
Sing a Nu Song
Together in Worship
7 Days
Crossroads
Lost and Found
Super Natural

Nu Hymnz: Live from the Motor City
Chain Breaker
This Is My Story
Live the Life

J. J. Hairston

You Deserve It
I See Victory
After This

Fred Hammond

Worship Journal
I Will Trust
United Tenors
God, Love & Romance
Life in the Word
Love Unstoppable
Free to Worship
Somethin' 'bout Love
Speak Those Things: POL Chapter 3
Christmas…Just Remember
Purpose by Design
Pages of Life: Chapters I & II
The Spirit of David
The Inner Court
Deliverance
I Am Persuaded

Tramaine Hawkins

Gospel Legacy
My Everything
I Never Lost My Praise
Still Tramaine
To a Higher Place
Live
The Joy That Floods My Soul
The Search Is Over
20th Century Masters—The Millennium
    Collection: The Best of Tramaine
    Hawkins

Israel Houghton

Covered: Alive in Asia
Jesus at the Center: Live
Decade
Love God. Love People.
    (The London Sessions)
The Power of One
A Deeper Level
A Timeless Christmas
Alive in South Africa
Live from Another Level
Real
New Season (Live)
Nueva Generación
Whisper It Loud

Keith "Wonderboy" Johnson

Back 2 Basics Chapter Two
Stronger than Ever
Just Being Me
Unity
Our Gift to You
New Season
Send a Revival
Tribute to Quartet Legends, Vol. 1
Would You
Live and Alive
Through the Storm

Le'Andria Johnson

The Experience
The Evolution of Le'Andria Johnson

Canton Jones

I Am Justice
God City USA
Lust, Drugs & Gospel
C.J. Talks
Kingdom Business 4
Dominionaire
Kingdom Business, Pt. 3
Kingdom Business, Pt. 2
Kingdom Business

The Password: Access Granted
Love Jones
20 Yrs. 3 Mths. & 12 Days…

John P. Kee

Yes Lord
There Is Hope
Wash Me
Churchin'
We Walk by Faith
Lilies in the Valley
Color Blind
Just Me This Time
Never Shall Forget
Wait on Him
Show Up!
Stand!
A Special Christmas Gift
Thursday Love
Strength
Any Day
Not Guilty… The Experience
Blessed by Association
The Color of Music
Live at the Fellowship
The Legacy Project
Life & Favor
Level Next

Deon Kipping

Something to Talk About
I Just Want to Hear You
Real Life. Real Worship.

Mary Mary

Something Big
The Sound
A Mary Mary Christmas
Mary Mary
Incredible
Thankful

Donnie McClurkin

The Journey (Live)
Duets
We All Are One (Live in
    Detroit)
Psalms, Hymns and Spiritual
    Songs
Donnie McClurkin Again
Live in London and More

William McDowell

Sounds of Revival, Pt. 2
Sounds of Revival
Withholding Nothing

Arise: The Live Worship
    Experience
As We Worship Live

VaShawn Mitchell

Secret Place
Unstoppable
Created 4 This
Triumphant
Promises
Believe in Your Dreams
So Satisfied

J. Moss

GFG Reload
Grown Folks Gospel
V4...The Other Side
Just James
V2...
The J Moss Project

William Murphy

Demonstrate
God Chaser
We Are One
The Sound
All Day

Jason Nelson

Jesus Revealed
Shifting the Atmosphere
Place of Worship
I Shall Live

Charisse Nelson-McIntosh

Broken, Vol. 2: Live (with William Becton)
Thank You for the Change (with Youthful Praise)
Promises (with Richard Smallwood and Vision)

Smokie Norful

Forever Yours
In the Meantime
How I Got Over…Songs That Carried Us
Smokie Norful Presents Victory Cathedral Choir
Live
Life Changing
Nothing without You
Limited Edition
I Need You Now

Worship & a Word: Matters of the Heart
Worship & a Word: According to Your Faith
Worship & a Word: The Myth of Unmet Needs

Kelly Price

Kelly
This Is Who I Am
Priceless
One Family: A Christmas Album
Mirror Mirror
Soul of a Woman

Hart Ramsey

True Story
Next Now!
My Next Heartbeat
Charge It to My Heart

Marvin Sapp

You Shall Live
Christmas Card
I Win
Here I Am
Thirsty

Be Exalted
Diary of a Psalmist
I Believe
Nothing Else Matters
Grace & Mercy
Marvin Sapp

Karen Clark Sheard

Destined to Win
All in One
It's Not Over
The Heavens Are Telling
2nd Chance
Finally Karen

Kierra Sheard

Graceland
Free
Bold Right Life
This Is Me
Just Until…
I Owe You

Richard Smallwood

Promises
The Center of My Joy

Journey: Live in New York
Persuaded: Live in D.C.
Healing: Live in Detroit
Rejoice
Adoration: Live in Atlanta
Live
Testimony
Vision
Portrait
Textures
Richard Smallwood Singers

Micah Stampley

To the King…Vertical Worship
Love Never Fails
One Voice
Release Me
Ransomed
A Fresh Wind…The Second Sound
The Songbook of Micah

Kathy Taylor

Live: The Worship Experience

Tonéx

Unspoken
Oak Park 921'06
Out the Box
O2
The Hostile Takeover
Pronounced Toe-Nay

Tye Tribbett

Greater Than
Fresh
Life (with G.A.)

Trin-i-tee 5:7

Angel & Chanelle
Love, Peace, Joy at Christmas
T57
The Kiss
Spiritual Love
Trin-I-Tee 5:7

Uncle Reece

Bold

Hezekiah Walker

Azusa, The Next Generation 2: Better
Azusa, The Next Generation
Souled Out
Family Affair II: Live at Radio City Music Hall
Love Is Live!
Family Affair
Recorded Live at Love Fellowship Tabernacle
Live in London at Wembley
Live in New York: By Any Means…
Live in Atlanta at Morehouse College
Live in Toronto
Focus on Glory
Oh Lord We Praise You
I'll Make It

The Walls Group

Fast Forward

Melvin Williams

Love like Crazy
Crazy like Love
Never Seen Your Face
Live in Memphis II

Back to the Cross
In Living Color "Live"

Michelle Williams

Journey to Freedom
Unexpected
Do You Know
Heart to Yours

BeBe Winans

America America
Cherch
Dream
My Christmas Prayer
BeBe Live and Up Close
Love & Freedom
BeBe Winans
Relationships (with CeCe Winans)

CeCe Winans

Let Them Fall in Love
Songs of Emotional Healing
Thy Kingdom Come
CeCe Winans Presents Pure Worship
CeCe Winans Presents Kingdom Kidz
Purified
Throne Room

CeCe Winans
Alabaster Box
His Gift
Everlasting Love
Alone in His Presence

Marvin Winans

The Praise + Worship
   Experience
Alone but Not Alone
The Songs of Marvin
   Winans
Friends

Vickie Winans

How I Got Over
Happy Holidays
Woman to Woman: Songs of Life
My Christmas Gift to You
Bringing It All Together
Share the Laughter
Live in Detroit, Vol. 2
Live in Detroit
Vickie Winans
The Lady
Total Victory
Be Encouraged

Praise ye the LORD.

Praise God in His sanctuary:

Praise Him in the firmament of His power.

Praise Him for His mighty acts:

Praise Him according to His excellent greatness.

Praise Him with the sound of the trumpet:

Praise Him with the psaltery and harp.

Praise Him with the timbrel and dance:

Praise Him with stringed instruments and organs.

Praise Him upon the loud cymbals:

Praise Him upon the high sounding cymbals.

Let every thing that hath breath praise the LORD.

Praise ye the LORD.

—Psalm 150 (KJV)

About the Authors

Carol M. Mackey is the former editor in chief of Black Expressions Book Club, the largest direct-to-consumer book club for African Americans in the nation. Under Mackey's editorial leadership, Black Expressions was voted Book Club of the Year by the African American Literary Awards Show for eight years during her tenure.

Widely recognized as a leading expert on African American literature, Mackey was named among the 50 Most Powerful African Americans in Publishing by *Black Issues Book Review* and has been featured in *Literary Divas: The Top 100+ Most Admired African-American Women in Literature*, a compilation of biographies about African American women who have powerfully impacted America's literary history. An engaging on-air guest, she has appeared on several segments of CBS TV's morning news show, C-Span, YouTube, and public television and was often interviewed by other media outlets on the state of African American publishing.

She is the author of the best-selling *Sistergirl Devotions: Keeping Jesus in the Mix on the Job*, published by Revell Books. Mackey was voted the 2010 Breakout Author of the Year at the African American Literary Awards Show. *Sistergirl Devotions* was named "Best Book to Take to Work" by *Ebony Magazine* (March 2012).

She lives in New York.

B. Jeffrey Grant-Clark is truly a music man. From his personal life to his career choices, music has been an integral part of his life. Grant, like most, got his start in music in the church. An accomplished keyboardist, he grew up playing in the church, which in fact set up a foundation for his life and musical career. His anointing and talent led him to play for various local churches in his home-

town of Buffalo, New York. Eventually, in an auspicious move to Detroit, Michigan, Grant had the opportunity to play for the legendary Dr. Mattie Moss Clark for several years.

During his time with Dr. Clark, he was bitten by the "radio bug," which led to a move back home to Buffalo, where he spent time on the air at WUFO. Honing his on-air talents, Grant listened to such influencers of the day as Frankie Crocker, Jerry Bledsoe, Don Allen Jr., Keith Pollard, Byron Pitts, and Gary Byrd. Grant spent sixteen years as program director and morning announcer at several stations in the Northeast / Ohio Valley region.

Throughout his career in radio, he also evolved into a proficient music producer and songwriter. His credits include coproducing for the gospel group Charisma and writing for several artists including Hezekiah Walker.

Grant's expertise in music led him to the next phase in his career. He served a brief stint at GRP Records, working with artists like Chick Corea, George Benson, David Benoit, and Dave Grusin. From there he went on to become the Northeast promotions manager at Warner Bros. Records in New York City, where he was largely responsible for the promotions

(continued on next page)

of superstar artists like Prince, Chaka Khan, Karyn White, Maze, George Duke, and Joe Sample, among others.

In 1996, Grant chose to return to his gospel roots when he joined the then new gospel label Verity Records. For eighteen years, Grant contributed to the extraordinary growth of the label, becoming the number one purveyor of recorded gospel music in the country. He served as the vice president of radio promotions and artist relations for the label, which is now RCA Inspiration.

Grant is honored to have been instrumental in the successful careers of top gospel artists including Donnie McClurkin, Kirk Franklin, Fred Hammond, Hezekiah Walker, Jason Nelson, Richard Smallwood, Marvin Sapp, Le'Andria Johnson, Israel Houghton, Tasha Page-Lockhart, the Walls Group, Kurt Carr, Deon Kipping, William Murphy, Travis Greene, and many more. His anointing and talent led him around the world. Grant has gone from inside man, playing and writing for legendary artists, to company man, programming radio stations and serving as record label executive.

Always drawn to taking pictures and understanding composition and structure, Grant's love of photography began, like many hobbyists, with his immediate surroundings, family, and friends. One day he brought his camera to "work" on a routine radio visit with an artist, and a career was born.

Grant poured himself into his new passion. Studying and honing his craft, he began bringing his camera to more shows and events. His enthusiasm for shooting grew as did the response to his well-crafted photographs. He was afforded the opportunity to shoot gospel music's top recording artists in raw and unfiltered settings. Grant's photographs reveal vulnerable, impromptu, moving, and private moments and capture the essence of the artist.

Grant-Clark is happily married to a wonderful woman, Annette, and father to three "kidults"—Dawn, Damone, and Melanie—and grandfather to four girls, Madison, Morgan, Mia, and McKenzie, and the latest grand addition, grandson Samuel Benjamin.

But the hour is coming, and now is, when the true worshipers will worship the Father in spirit and truth; for the Father is seeking such to worship Him.

—John 4:23

Some trust in chariots, and some in horses, but we will remember the name of the LORD our God.

—Psalm 20:7

Oh, worship the LORD in the beauty of holiness! Tremble before Him, all the earth.

—Psalm 96:9

But thanks be to God, who gives us the victory through our Lord Jesus Christ.

—I Corinthians 15:57

"Allow the children to come to me," Jesus said. "Don't forbid them, because the kingdom of heaven belongs to people like these children."

—Matthew 19:14 (CEB)

31192021378946